The Little Giant® Book of American Presidents

Glen Vecchione

Illustrated by Maura Condrick

Sterling Publishing Co., Inc.
New York

Edited by Jeanette Green
Designed by Paul Richer and Lisa Stokes
Proofread by Lisa Smith

Library of Congress Cataloging-in-Publication Data

Vecchione, Glen.
  The little giant book of American presidents / Glen Vecchione;
  illustrated by Maura Condrick.
     p. cm.
  Includes index.
  ISBN-13: 978-1-4027-2692-7
  ISBN-10: 1-4027-2692-9
  1. Presidents—United States—Miscellanea—Juvenile literature. I.
  Condrick, Maura. II. Title.

E176.8.V43 2007
973.09'9--dc22   2006017349

2   4   6   8   10   9   7   5   3   1

Published by Sterling Publishing Co., Inc.
387 Park Avenue South, New York, NY 10016
© 2007 by Glen Vecchione
Distributed in Canada by Sterling Publishing
c/o Canadian Manda Group, 165 Dufferin Street
Toronto, Ontario, Canada M6K 3H6
Distributed in the United Kingdom by GMC Distribution Services
Castle Place, 166 High Street, Lewes, East Sussex, England BN7 1XU
Distributed in Australia by Capricorn Link (Australia) Pty. Ltd.
P.O. Box 704, Windsor, NSW 2756, Australia

Printed in China
All rights reserved

Sterling ISBN-13: 978-1-4027-2692-7
ISBN-10: 1-4027-2692-9

For information about custom editions, special sales, premium and
corporate purchases, please contact Sterling Special Sales
Department at 800-805-5489 or specialsales@sterlingpub.com.

Contents

Introduction

American presidents have been a colorful group of men—some privileged and others self-made—who have shown the rest of the world that Americans were a hard-working, practical people; a people who wanted sensible solutions to the problems of the country. After all, ours was a nation founded on ideals of liberty, equality, and justice; a country detached from the rule of royal tyrants and the troubling politics of religious beliefs.

Our leaders reflected this. Many were down-to-earth, robust, and forthright. Others were anything but that. And while European aristocracy delighted in the parlor banter of Thomas Jefferson, it shuddered at the moose head hanging in Teddy Roosevelt's State Dining Room. Such was the nature and style of our uniquely American government.

The Little Giant Book® of American Presidents takes you on a journey through the times and lives of our leaders—all 43 of them. As you turn these pages, we hope that you will learn things you never knew. Here are just a few tidbits.

★ Ulysses S. Grant was the first and only president to get a speeding ticket while in office. He was driving a horse and buggy.
★ Andrew Jackson was the first to have running water piped into the White House.
★ Calvin Coolidge was so fond of roasted chicken that he had a chicken coop installed behind the White house.

We hope that these and other little-known facts about the men who occupied the highest office in the land will delight you for years to come. We also know that a book like this is never finished. Historians, it seems, continue to discover new details about past presidents while the media constantly dog recent ones. Future historians may even have women presidents to write about. After all, women have held the highest office for nearly every major world power, except the United States.

Here are the men who have served America as its chief executive from the late 18th to the early 21st century.

Chronological List of American Presidents

1   George Washington (1789–1797)
2   John Adams (1797–1801)
3   Thomas Jefferson (1801–1809)
4   James Madison (1809–1817)
5   James Monroe (1817–1825)
6   John Quincy Adams (1825–1829)
7   Andrew Jackson (1829–1837)
8   Martin Van Buren (1837–1841)
9   William Henry Harrison (March 4–April 4, 1841)
10 John Tyler (1841–1845)
11 James Knox Polk (1845–1849)
12 Zachary Taylor (1849–1850)
13 Millard Fillmore (1850–1853)
14 Franklin Pierce (1853–1857)
15 James Buchanan (1857–1861)
16 Abraham Lincoln (1861–1865)
17 Andrew Johnson (1865–1869)
18 Ulysses Simpson Grant (1869–1877)
19 Rutherford Birchard Hayes (1877–1881)
20 James Abram Garfield (March–September 1881)

21	Chester Alan Arthur (1881–1885)
22	(Stephen) Grover Cleveland (1885–1889)
23	Benjamin Harrison (1889–1893)
24	Grover Cleveland (1893–1897)
25	William McKinley (1897–1901)
26	Theodore Roosevelt (Teddy) (1901–1909)
27	William Howard Taft (1909–1913)
28	(Thomas) Woodrow Wilson (1913–1921)
29	Warren Gamaliel Harding (1921–1923)
30	(John) Calvin Coolidge (1923–1929)
31	Herbert Clark Hoover (1929–1933)
32	Franklin Delano Roosevelt (1933–1945)
33	Harry S. Truman (1945–1953)
34	Dwight David Eisenhower (Ike) (1953–1961)
35	John Fitzgerald Kennedy (1961–1963)
36	Lyndon Baines Johnson (1963–1969)
37	Richard Milhous Nixon (1969–1974)
38	Gerald Rudolph Ford (1974–1977)
39	James Earl Carter, Jr. (Jimmy) (1977–1981)
40	Ronald Wilson Reagan (1981–1989)
41	George Herbert Walker Bush (1989–1993)
42	William Jefferson Clinton (Bill) (1993–2001)
43	George Walker Bush (2001–)

Alphabetical List of American Presidents

Adams, John
Adams, John Quincy
Arthur, Chester A.
Buchanan, James
Bush, George H. W.
Bush, George W.
Carter, James E.
Coolidge, Calvin
Cleveland, Grover
Clinton, William Jefferson
Eisenhower, Dwight D.
Fillmore, Millard
Ford, Gerald R.
Garfield, James A.
Grant, Ulysses S.
Harding, Warren G.
Harrison, Benjamin
Harrison, William Henry
Hayes, Rutherford B.
Hoover, Herbert
Jackson, Andrew

Jefferson, Thomas
Johnson, Andrew
Johnson, Lyndon B.
Kennedy, John F.
Lincoln, Abraham
Madison, James
McKinley, William
Monroe, James
Nixon, Richard M.
Pierce, Franklin
Polk, James K.
Reagan, Ronald
Roosevelt, Franklin D.
Roosevelt, Theodore
Taft, William H.
Taylor, Zachary
Truman, Harry S.
Tyler, John
Van Buren, Martin
Washington, George
Wilson, Woodrow

Chapter I
Presidential Timeline

American presidents were mostly practical men for their times—they saw problems and tried to fix them. Or they saw opportunities and acted. Some presidents were flexible and responsive; others were rigid and seemed out of touch. Some were keen observers of the world stage; others preferred their own backyards. Each followed his heart and did the best he could.

The Earliest Congressional "Presidents"
(1774–1788)

The first and second Continental Congress and the United States in Congress Assembled meet in Philadelphia with representatives from the Thirteen Colonies. A series of 15 "presidents" preside. Their role was akin to that of today's Speaker of the House of Representatives. (1774–1788)

On April 1, 1774, the Boston Tea Party sets off the conflict with Great Britain. Massachusetts patriots, dressed as Mohawks, dump crates of tea from ships into Boston Harbor in defiance of the taxes exacted by Great Britain. King George III and Parliament close the port. (1774)

The First Continental Congress convenes in Philadelphia from September 5, 1774, to October 26, 1774, and two presidents serve.

The American War for Independence begins when the first shots are fired at Lexington and Concord, Massachusetts, in April 1775.

The Second Continental Congress meets from May 10, 1775, to March 1, 1781, and five presidents serve.

George Washington takes command of the Continental Army. The American Revolutionary War achieves the United States' independence from Great Britain. (1775–1783)

Thomas Paine publishes the pamphlet *Common Sense,* January 1776.

Thomas Jefferson drafts the Declaration of Independence, which is ratified by Congress on July 2, 1776, and published July 4, 1776.

Congress ratifies the Articles of Confederation (the Constitution). (1781)

The United States in Congress Assembled meets from March 1, 1781, to November 2, 1788. Ten men, including John Hancock, serve as presidents for the various sessions.

State delegates meet in Philadelphia to draft a new Constitution in 1787, and the Constitution is ratified by the 13 states. (1788)

George Washington is chosen to be the first president of the United States of America. (1789)

During the Presidency of George Washington (1789–1797)

Congress creates the U.S. State Department, War Department, Treasury Department, and Supreme Court between July and September 1789. The first Congress meets at Federal Hall, New York City, on March 4th, 1789.

The French Revolution begins with the storming of the Bastille, a former prison, used to stock munitions, in July 1789.

The first census is undertaken, revealing a population of just under 4 million. (1790)

In 1789, James Madison introduces the first twelve amendments to the U.S. Constitution. Ten of the twelve are ratified in 1791. Today they're known as the Bill of Rights that guarantee essential rights and liberties omitted in the original drafting of the Constitution.

George Washington
(1789–1797)

Construction begins on the White House, based on plans by Irish-American architect James Hoban. (1792)

Eli Whitney invents the cotton gin, a device that increases the demand for slave labor over the coming decades. (1793)

15

The United States pays $1 million in ransom to pirates from North Africa (Barbary Coast) for the release of 115 seamen. (1795) The ransom is followed by years of annual tributes to keep the pirates from attacking U.S. vessels.

The artist Gilbert Stuart creates the portrait of Washington that appears today on the $1 bill. (1795)

During the Presidency of John Adams (1797–1801)

The warships the *U.S.S. United States, U.S.S. Constellation*, and *U.S.S. Constitution* ("Old Ironsides") are launched, followed by the founding of the Department of the Navy and the Marine Corps. (1797)

The Alien and Seditions Acts are enacted in an attempt to silence political opposition. (1798)

Napoleon comes to power in France and rules as a dictator. (1799)

Napoleon's soldiers discover the Rosetta Stone in Egypt, which leads to the translation of Egyptian hieroglyphics. (1799)

George Washington dies at his Mount Vernon estate. (1799)

The Library of Congress is created in 1800 with an act of Congress providing for purchase of books and an apartment to contain them. Thomas Jefferson later donates his library, and the foundation for the Library of Congress is laid in 1815.

John Adams
(1797–1801)

The nation's capital moves from Philadelphia to Washington, D.C., and John Adams and his wife Abigail are the first occupants of the executive mansion. (1800)

During the Presidency of Thomas Jefferson (1801–1809)

West Point is founded along the upper Hudson River in New York. (1802)

The Louisiana Purchase doubles the size of the United States. (1803)

English chemist John Dalton introduces the theory that all matter is made from atoms. (1803)

Jefferson orders Lewis and Clark to explore the Northwest United States. (1804)

Vice President Aaron Burr shoots Alexander Hamilton, first secretary of the treasury, in a duel at Weehawken, New Jersey. (1804)

The first steam locomotive is built by English engineer Richard Trevithick and demonstrated in Wales. (1804)

Noah Webster publishes *A Compendious Dictionary of the English Language* in 1806. He begins work on *An American Dictionary of the English Language* with 70,000 entries, published in 1828, which surpasses Samuel Johnson's 1755 English masterpiece.

The American inventor Robert Fulton makes the first steamboat trip from New York City to Albany. (1807)

African slave trade to the U.S. ends. (1808)

Thomas Jefferson
(1801–1809)

During the Presidency of James Madison (1809–1817)

Construction begins on the Cumberland Road, the first national highway. The road starts in Maryland, becoming an important route to the western United States. (1811)

James Madison
(1809–1817)

Over 400 slaves revolt in the state of Louisiana, killing the son of a plantation owner, burning crops, and marching toward New Orleans. About 90 slaves die; many are decapitated and their heads put on posts along the River Road as a warning to other slaves. (1811)

The War of 1812—between the United States and Britain—begins on June 18, 1812, and ends in 1815.

Francis Scott Key writes "The Star-Spangled Banner" while watching the British attack Baltimore on the night of September 13 during the War of 1812. Congress does not adopt it as the official national anthem until March 3, 1931.

British troops burn buildings in Washington, D.C., including the White House, forcing President Madison, his family, and Congress to flee Washington, D.C., in August 1814.

A U.S. flotilla finally eliminates piracy against U.S. vessels by destroying rogue ships from the Barbary Coast (North Africa). (1815)

The first public school for the deaf is established in Hartford, Connecticut. (1817)

During the Presidency of James Monroe (1817–1825)

Mississippi becomes a state. (1817)

The novel *Frankenstein* is published by English author Mary Wollstonecraft Shelley. (1818)

Spain surrenders Florida to the United States. (1819)

Three states—Connecticut, Massachusetts, and New York—expand voting rights by eliminating property-ownership qualifications. (1821)

The nation's first public high school opens in Boston, Massachusetts. (1821)

Yale College bans football, citing its violence and tendency to distract from serious academic study. (1822)

President Monroe declares that U.S. foreign policy will oppose European intervention in American affairs. The policy becomes known as the *Monroe Doctrine*. (1823)

James Monroe
(1817–1825)

During the Presidency of John Quincy Adams (1825–1829)

Ludwig van Beethoven's Symphony No. 9 is performed in Vienna. (1824)

The Erie Canal opens, connecting the Hudson River and Lake Erie, and launches the economic development of the Midwest, especially the areas around the Great Lakes. (1825)

James Fenimore Cooper publishes *The Last of the Mohicans.* (1826)

Thomas Jefferson and John Adams both die on July 4, 1826.

John Quincy Adams
(1825–1829)

During the Presidency of Andrew Jackson (1829–1837)

Electromagnetism is discovered simultaneously by physicists Michael Faraday of England and Joseph Henry of the United States. (1830)

The Baltimore and Ohio, the first American passenger train, begins service. (1830)

The Indian Removal Act forces Native Americans to resettle in the American West. (1830)

Joseph Smith publishes the *Book of Mormon* and founds the Church of Jesus Christ of Latter-Day Saints in Fayette, New York. (1830)

Andrew Jackson
(1829–1837)

The Virginia slave Nat Turner leads a slave revolt resulting in the deaths of 57 whites and 100 slaves. (1831)

The Liberty Bell is cracked while tolling the death of Chief Justice John Marshall. (1835)

Texas declares its independence from Mexico. (1836)

Ralph Waldo Emerson's first book, *Nature*, is published. (1836)

During the Presidency of Martin Van Buren (1837–1841)

American Samuel F. B. Morse invents the telegraph. (1837)

England's Queen Victoria begins a 63-year reign. (1837)

Frederick Douglass escapes from slavery and begins to become a key leader in the abolitionist movement. (1838)

Over 16,000 Cherokee Indian people are forced to relocate from their homelands in Georgia, North Carolina, Tennessee, Alabama, and other states to the Indian Territory (today known as Oklahoma) during the infamous Trail of Tears. (1838)

Abner Doubleday develops the rules for the new game of baseball. (1839)

Immigration increases the population of the United States to nearly 17 million. (1840)

The first wagon train leaves Independence, Missouri, for California. It transports 47 people, taking seven months to complete the journey. (1841)

Martin Van Buren
(1837–1841)

Edgar Allan Poe publishes one of the first American detective stories, *The Murders in the Rue Morgue*. (1841)

During the Presidency of William Henry Harrison (1841)

The Supreme Court allows the slave mutineers—who in 1839 took over the ship the *Amistad*—to return to their homes in Africa. (1841)

During the Presidency of John Tyler (1841–1845)

William Henry Harrison
(March 4–April 4, 1841)

The first child labor laws are passed in England. (1840s)

Anesthesia is used for the first time during surgery on a patient, in Boston, Massachusetts. (1842)

The Webster-Ashburton Treaty fixes the U.S.-Canadian border in Maine and Minnesota. (1842) The settlement of Oregon begins with an informal northbound hiking path, which soon broadens to become the Oregon Trail. (1843)

Samuel Morse sends the first telegraph message, "What has God wrought," from Washington to Baltimore. (1844)

Texas becomes a state. (1845)

John Tyler
(1841–1845)

During the Presidency of James K. Polk (1845–1849)

The Irish Potato Famine begins, provoking a wave of Irish emigrants to U.S. shores. (1845)

Edgar Allan Poe publishes *The Raven and Other Poems*. (1845)

After violent clashes with settlers over polygamy, the Mormons leave Illinois and settle in Salt Lake City, Utah. (1845)

Elias Howe patents the sewing machine. (1846)

The first five-cent and ten-cent adhesive postage stamps are sold. They feature pictures of Benjamin Franklin and George Washington. (1847)

James Knox Polk
(1845–1849)

Gold is discovered at Sutter's Mill in California, triggering the California Gold Rush. (1848)

The treaty of Guadalupe Hidalgo cuts Mexico's size in half and increases that of the United States by one third. The annexed terroitory ceded by Mexico covers what become the future states of California, Neveda, Utah, and parts of Arizona, New Mexico, Colorado and Wyoming. (1848)

During the Presidency of Zachary Taylor (1849–1850)

Elizabeth Blackwell becomes the first female to graduate from a medical school in the United States. (1849)

Harriet Tubman escapes slavery in Maryland in 1849 and settles in Philadelphia. She later becomes an active abolitionist, participating in the Underground Railroad, which gives refuge to escaping slaves.

Nathanial Hawthorne writes the

Zachary Taylor
(1849–1850)

30

novel *The Scarlet Letter*, which immediately becomes the best-selling book of its time. (1850)

The Santa Fe stagecoach route is created to carry mail between Independence, Missouri, and Santa Fe, New Mexico. (1850)

During the Presidency of Millard Fillmore (1850–1853)

California is admitted to the Union as a free state (slavery is prohibited). (1850)

The Fugitive Slave Act is passed, stipulating harsh punishments for escaped slaves. (1850)

American author Harriet Beecher Stowe begins publishing weekly

Millard Fillmore
(1850–1853)

installments of *Uncle Tom's Cabin* in a Maine abolitionist magazine. (1851)

Herman Melville publishes *Moby-Dick*, the first novel about men pursuing whales. (1851)

Massachusetts enacts legislation that requires children to attend school. (1852)

Political cartoonist Thomas Nast produces the first Uncle Sam character based on meat-packer Samuel Wilson. Legend has it that Wilson's U.S. stamp on his meat came to be known as Uncle Sam, symbolizing the federal government. (1852)

During the Presidency of Franklin Pierce (1853–1857)

New York is the first U.S. city to host a World's Fair. (1853)

Composer Stephen Foster in 1853 publishes the song "My Old Kentucky Home, Good-Night!" that romanticizes plantation life. The lyrics were later modified.

American naval officer Commodore Matthew Perry arrives in Japan to establish trade between the United States and Japan. For two centuries, only the Chinese and the Dutch had been admitted in Japanese ports. The Japanese described the ships as "giant dragons puffing smoke." (1853)

The Republican Party is created after the Kansas-Nebraska Act, which opens the territories (within the Louisiana Purchase) to slavery. (1854)

The Republican Party is created in part to oppose slavery as set forth in the Kansas-Nebraska Act. (1854)

Franklin Pierce
(1853–1857)

Henry David Thoreau's book *Walden, or Life in the Woods* is published. (1854)

Walt Whitman's collection of poems, *Leaves of Grass*, is published. (1855)

The first kindergarten is established in Watertown, Wisconsin. (1856)

During the Presidency of James Buchanan (1857–1861)

The Supreme Court ruling on the Dred Scott decision stipulates that Congress cannot prohibit slavery in the territories and that African-Americans do not have citizenship rights. (1857)

The first popular Currier & Ives print, *Trotting Cracks on the Snow*, is printed. (1858)

The first Otis elevator, invented by Elisha G. Otis, is installed at 488 Broadway in New York. (1857)

The transatlantic cable is completed by Cyrus W. Field. (1858)

Abolitionist John Brown fails in his attempt to incite a slave revolt by attacking the U.S. arsenal at Harpers Ferry in Virginia. (1859)

Georgia passes a law that forbids slave owners to free slaves in their wills. (1859)

The Pony Express is created using a relay system to carry mail from Missouri to California. (1860)

South Carolina secedes from the Union, followed by Mississippi, Florida, and Alabama. (1860)

James Buchanan
(1857–1861)

During the Presidency of Abraham Lincoln (1861–1865)

The Civil War begins as Confederate troops attack Fort Sumter in Charleston, South Carolina, capturing it in five weeks. (1861)

Telegraph lines link New York City and San Francisco. (1861)

The Homestead Act grants free farms to settlers. (1862)

The Morrill Land Grant Act (1862) provides public land for use in (agricultural and engineering) education. Later acts helped create land-grant colleges and universities.

Abraham Lincoln issues the Emancipation Proclamation on September 23, 1862. It grants freedom to slaves within states

Abraham Lincoln
(1861–1865)

still in rebellion by January 1, 1863. No Confederate states accept the offer.

During the Civil War, Congress passes a military draft, which provokes four days of riots in New York City, resulting in more than 1,000 casualties. Members of the working class are outraged that wealthy people could pay poor folk to take their places in the military. (1863)

On November 19, 1863, Abraham Lincoln delivers the Gettysburg Address at the Soldiers' National Cemetery in Gettysburg, Pennsylvania. At the Battle of Gettysburg four and a half months earlier, over 7,500 people and nearly as many horses died.

President Abraham Lincoln revives the celebration of Thanksgiving Day by appointing the last Thursday in November as a national holiday. (1863)

Union General William Tecumseh Sherman marches through Georgia, taking Atlanta and Savannah. (1864)

Confederate General Robert E. Lee surrenders at Appomattox Court House in Virginia, ending the Civil War. (1865)

During the Presidency of Andrew Johnson (1865–1869)

The Thirteenth Amendment, abolishing slavery, is ratified on December 6, 1865.

Lewis Carroll publishes *Alice's Adventures Underground*. (1865)

The Ku Klux Klan forms in the South to terrorize African-Americans. (1866)

Congress approves the minting of a new coin, nicknamed the "nickel." (1866)

Andrew Johnson
(1865–1869)

Christopher Latham Sholes, an editor and printer from Milwaukee, invents the typewriter. (1867)

Russia sells Alaska to the U.S. for $7.2 million. (1867)

The Fourteenth Amendment, providing citizenship to all former slaves, is ratified. (1869)

During the Presidency of Ulysses S. Grant (1869–1877)

The transcontinental railroad is completed and celebrated with a golden spike driven at Promontory Summit, Utah. The spike marks the meeting of the Central Pacific with the Union Pacific. (1869)

Susan B. Anthony and Elizabeth Cady Stanton found and lead the

Ulysses Simpson Grant
(1869–1877)

National Woman Suffrage Association, dedicated to helping women secure the right to vote. (1869)

The first national trade union, the Knights of Labor, forms in Philadelphia. (1869)

The Fifteenth Amendment, guaranteeing African-Americans the right to vote, is ratified. (1870)

A fire that begins in a barn, where Patrick and Catherine O'Leary's cow reportedly kicked over a lantern, spreads to consume the wooden buildings in Chicago. In four days, hundreds of people die and nearly 100,000 are left homeless. (1871)

Joseph Glidden invents barbed wire, which ends the era of the open prairie in the American West. (1873)

 Alexander Graham Bell invents the telephone. (1876)

During the Presidency of Rutherford B. Hayes (1877–1881)

U.S. troops suppress a national railroad strike. (1877)

Thomas A. Edison creates the Edison Electric Light Company. (1878)

Coca-Cola is first sold at Jacob's Pharmacy in Atlanta, Georgia. (1878)

F. W. Woolworth opens the first successful five-and-ten-cent store in Lancaster, Pennsylvania. His five-cent store, opened in Utica, New York, failed within weeks. (1879)

Electricity is used to light selected public thoroughfares in New York City. (1880)

Rutherford Birchard Hayes
(1877–1881)

The Supreme Court declares that income tax laws are unconstitutional. (1881)

During the Presidency of James A. Garfield (1881)

The American Red Cross is founded. (1881)

Booker T. Washington founds the Tuskegee Institute, a school for African-Americans. (1881)

A gunfight between Wyatt Earp and his men and cattle rustlers takes place at the OK Corral in Tombstone, Arizona. (1881)

Returning from exile in Canada with the starving Lakota people, Sioux Chief Sitting Bull surrenders to U.S. authorities. (1881)

James Abram Garfield
(March–September 1881)

During the Presidency of Chester A. Arthur (1881–1885)

Congress passes the Chinese Exclusion Act, one of a series of immigration laws, which effectively bans Chinese immigration to the U.S. until 1943. (1882)

The Brooklyn Bridge opens, linking the boroughs of Manhattan and Brooklyn. (1883)

Mark Twain's masterpiece, *The Adventures of Huckleberry Finn*, is published. (1884)

The first roller coaster opens at Coney Island in Brooklyn, New York. (1884)

The first skyscraper, the Home Insurance Building (a ten-story building

Chester Alan Arthur
(1881–1885)

supported by a metal skeleton), is completed in Chicago. (1885)

The Washington Monument is opened to the public after 36 years of construction. (1885)

During the Presidency of Grover Cleveland (1885–1889 and 1893–1897)

The Haymarket Riots break out in Chicago, resulting from the bitter disputes over an 8-hour work day. (1886)

The Statue of Liberty (named "Liberty Enlightening the World"), a gift from France to the United States, is dedicated in New York Harbor. (1886)

(Stephen) Grover Cleveland
(1885–1889)

The Apache leader Geronimo surrenders to U.S. troops in Skeleton Canyon, Arizona. (1886)

Congress declares Labor Day a national holiday, making the U.S. the first industrialized nation to celebrate its working population. (1894)
In Paris, France, Louis and Auguste Lumiere have the first public screening of a motion picture on December 28, 1895.

In the 1880s and 1890s, inventors tinkered with horseless carriages in Lansing, Dearborn, and Detroit, Michigan. Ransom Olds and Frank Clark created a gas-fired horseless carriage in 1887, and Henry Ford tests an automobile with a two-cylinder, air-cooled gasoline engine in 1896.

During the Presidency of Benjamin Harrison (1889–1893)

In Johnstown, Pennsylvania, a dam collapses and causes a flood that drowns 2,200 people. (1889)

French engineer Gustav Eiffel, who helped construct the Statue of Liberty, completes the Eiffel Tower for the Universal Exposition (World's Fair) in Paris, France. (1889)

On April 22, 1889, the U.S. opens Oklahoma to white settlement. Within 24 hours, 50,000 settlers claim 2 million acres.

At Wounded Knee Creek, South Dakota, U.S. troops kill Sitting Bull and more than 300 Sioux, many of them women and children. (1890)

Wyoming becomes a state; it is the first state to enter the Union that grants voting rights to women. (1890)

Electric lights are installed at the White House. (1891)

Benjamin Harrison
(1889–1893)

The mechanical zipper is patented by inventor Whitcomb Judson. (1891)

Ellis Island, the New York Harbor entry point for immigration, opens its doors. (1892)

During the Presidency of William McKinley (1897–1901)

After the discovery of gold in the Yukon Territory of Canada, the Klondike Gold Rush begins. (1897)

Polish scientist Marie Curie, née Sklodowska, and her husband, French scientist Pierre Curie, discover radium in 1898 in their Paris, France, laboratory. A few years later, they win the Nobel Prize.

William McKinley
(1897–1901)

The battleship *U.S.S. Maine* is sunk in Cuba's Havana harbor, which is one of the causes of the Spanish-American War. (1898)

Hawaii becomes a U.S. possession in 1898 and a territory in 1900.

Carrie Nation begins the Temperance League to discourage the sale and use of liquor. (1899)

On September 8, 1900, a hurricane in Galveston, Texas, kills one-sixth of the city's population—over 6,000 people.

During the Presidency of Theodore Roosevelt (1901–1909)

Orville and Wilbur Wright make their successful airplane flight at Kitty Hawk, North Carolina. (1903)

Roald Amundsen of Norway navigates through the dangerous Northwest Passage in the Arctic Ocean, linking Europe and Asia. (1903)

Albert Einstein introduces the theory of relativity. (1905)

Congress passes the Meat Inspection Act to clean up the unsanitary conditions rampant in the meat-packing industry, which Upton Sinclair exposes in the best-selling book *The Jungle*. (1906)

The San Francisco Earthquake, followed by four days of fire, kills 3,000 and causes $500 million in damage. (1906)

Theodore Roosevelt
(1901–1909)

Oklahoma becomes a state. (1907)

Ransom Olds establishes the first auto production plant in 1900, and Henry Ford introduces the mass-produced automobile, the Model T, in 1908.

During the Presidency of William Howard Taft (1909–1913)

The explorers Matthew Henson and Robert E. Peary reach the North Pole. (1909)

Father's Day is first celebrated in Spokane, Washington. (1910)

Norwegian explorer Roald Amundsen reaches the South Pole. (1911)
The British luxury liner, the *Titanic*, sinks in the North Atlantic Ocean. (1912)

New Mexico and Arizona become the 47th and 48th states, respectively. (1912)

Congress ratifies the Sixteenth Amendment, which creates a federal income tax. (1913)

William Howard Taft
(1909–1913)

During the Presidency of Woodrow Wilson (1913–1921)

The Panama Canal is completed. (1914)

The Great War, later known as World War I, begins in 1914 and lasts until 1918.

San Francisco and New York become the first two cities connected by telephone lines. (1915)

The Armistice ending World War I is signed on November 11, 1918.

The great flu epidemic kills nearly 40 million people worldwide, more than all the casualties of World War I. (1918)

(Thomas) Woodrow Wilson
(1913–1921)

Prohibition, detailed in the Eighteenth Amendment, making it illegal to manufacture, transport, and sell alcohol in the United States, goes into effect. (1920)

The Nineteenth Amendment gives women the right to vote. (1920)

During the Presidency of Warren G. Harding (1921–1923)

Immigration to the United States is restricted through the Emergency Quota Act of 1921 and later by an act in 1924. (1921)

The concept for the tomb of the Unknown Soldier, first created by the French to honor all the fallen soldiers of World War I, is adopted by the U.S. and established in Arlington National Cemetery in Virginia. (1921)

Warren Gamaliel Harding
(1921–1923)

Insulin is first used to treat diabetic patients. (1922)

English archeologist Howard Carter discovers the tomb of Egyptian King Tutankhamen (reign 1361–1352 B.C.). His name was later popularly shortened to "King Tut." (1922)

During the Presidency of Calvin Coolidge (1923–1929)

Jazz music begins to catch on in the upscale nightclubs of New Orleans and New York City, defying the spirit of segregation. (1920s)

Czech dramatist Karel Capek invents the word *robot*. (1923)

George Gershwin's symphonic jazz composition, *Rhapsody in Blue*, premiers. (1924)

Congress passes a law granting citizenship to Native Americans. (1924)

In a trial, John T. Scopes is found guilty for teaching evolution in a Dayton, Tennessee, high school. He is fined $100. (1925)

F. Scott Fitzgerald's novel *The Great Gatsby* is published. (1925)

Aviator Charles Lindbergh takes off from New York in 1927 and, with five sandwiches on board, lands in Paris, France, 33 hours later. His monumental achievement of flying nonstop across the Atlantic Ocean is celebrated worldwide. (1927)

(John) Calvin Coolidge
(1923–1929)

British microbiologist Alexander Fleming discovers penicillin. (1928)

During the Presidency of Herbert Hoover (1929–1933)

Aviator Amelia Earhart becomes the first woman to fly alone across the Atlantic Ocean. (1928)

The Great Depression begins with the collapse of the stock market. (1929)

Bell Laboratories begins experiments that lead to the development of color television. (1929)

The Empire State Building opens in New York City. (1931)

Construction begins on the Golden Gate Bridge in San Francisco. (1932)

Herbert Clark Hoover
(1929–1933)

During the Presidency of Franklin Delano Roosevelt (1933–1945)

The Twenty-first Amendment ends 13 years of Prohibition. (1933)

Congress passes a series of economic and social measures, known as the New Deal, to regulate banks, distribute funds to the jobless, create jobs, raise agricultural prices, and set wage and production standards for industry. (1934–1935)

Franklin Delano Roosevelt
(1933–1945)

Roosevelt signs a law creating the Securities and Exchange Commission. (1934)

The Works Progress Administration (WPA) is created to assist unemployed workers with training and job opportunities. (1935)

After much criticism and debate, the Social Security Act is passed by Congress to assist Americans in their retirement. (1935)

The German airship the *Hindenburg* explodes over Lakehurst, New Jersey. (1937)

Congress passes the first federal child labor laws. (1938)

Congress passes the Fair Labor Standards Act, which limits the working week to 40 hours. (1938)

John Steinbeck's novel *The Grapes of Wrath* is published, shocking Americans with its epic tale of a family impoverished and displaced by the Dust Bowl. (1939)

Under the direction of Hitler, German troops and later, Soviet troops from the east, invade Poland, provoking the outbreak of World War II. (1939)

After the bombing of Pearl Harbor on December 7, 1941, the United States declares war on Japan. This expands the fighting during World War II from the fronts in Europe and Africa to the Pacific.

During the Presidency of Harry S. Truman (1945–1953)

The United States drops the first atomic bombs on Hiroshima (August 6) and Nagasaki (August 9), bringing about the surrender of Japan on August 15, 1945.

In World War II, combat, disease, genocide, and aerial bombing of cities kill as many as 62 million people (accounts vary greatly). Italy surrenders in September 1943, Germany in May 1945, and Japan in August 1945. Americans celebrate V-E Day on May 7 and V-J Day on September 2 with the signing of peace agreements.

British Prime Minister Winston Churchill first uses the term *Iron Curtain* to describe the separation between capitalist Western Europe and Communist Eastern Europe. (1946)

The Soviet Union detonates its first atomic weapon. (1949)

America develops the hydrogen bomb (500 times more powerful than the atomic bomb) and tensions with the Soviet Union mount. (1949)

The country of Israel is founded. (1948)

The North Atlantic Treaty Organization (NATO) forms to defend Western Europe against a potential attack by the Communist Soviet Union. (1949)

Harry S. Truman
(1945–1953)

The United States becomes involved in the Korean War. (1950–1953)

The Twenty-second Amendment to the Constitution, limiting presidents to a maximum of two terms in office, is ratified. (1951)

During the Presidency of Dwight D. Eisenhower (1953–1961)

The Cold War heats up, as both the United States and Soviet Union test super-powerful hydrogen bombs. (1953)

The polio vaccine is developed by Jonas Salk. (1954)

Brown v. Board of Education bans segregation in public schools. (1954)

Dwight David Eisenhowe
(1953–1961)

In Montgomery, Alabama, an African-American, Rosa Parks, refuses to give up her seat in a bus to a white passenger, triggering the civil-rights movement. (1955)

Congress passes the Federal-Aid Highway Act, which helps create the interstate highway system. (1956)

Elvis Presley makes his first appearance on television. (1956)

After colliding with the Swedish luxury liner the *Stockholm*, the Italian cruise ship *Andrea Doria* sinks off the Long Island coast near Montauk, New York. (1956)

 Sputnik I and *II* are satellites launched by the Soviet Union, triggering the "Space Race." (1957)

Congress establishes the National Aeronautics and Space Administration (NASA). (1958)

Alaska and Hawaii become the 49th and 50th states, respectively. (1958 and 1959)

During the Presidency of John Fitzgerald Kennedy (1961–1963)

Reacting to Khrushchev's pledge of support to North Vietnam, the United States makes a commitment to contain communism in North Vietnam. (1961)

President John F. Kennedy creates the Peace Corps by executive order. (1961)

The U.S. sends 400 Green Berets as "special advisors" to South Vietnam to train South Vietnamese troops to fight against North Vietnamese troops. (1961)

John Fitzgerald Kennedy (1961–1963)

Alan B. Shepard, Jr., becomes the first American to fly into suborbital space. (1961)

East Germany constructs the Berlin Wall to divide East and West Berlin and prevent East Germans from fleeing Communist rule. (1961)

The Supreme Court rules that school prayer is unconstitutional because it violates the principle of separation between church and state. (1962)

President John F. Kennedy's stern position during the Cuban Missile Crisis forces the Soviet Union to abandon plans to install nuclear missiles in Cuba. (1962)

Rachel Carson's *Silent Spring* launches the environmentalist movement. (1962)

John Glenn, Jr., is the first American astronaut to orbit the Earth. (1963)

Martin Luther King, Jr., delivers his famous

"I Have a Dream" speech at the Lincoln Memorial in Washington, D.C. (1963)

The number of U.S. military advisors in South Vietnam reaches 16,300 and military aid exceeds $500 million. (1963)

On November 22, 1963, President Kennedy is assassinated in Dallas. The entire nation mourns.

During the Presidency of Lyndon Baines Johnson (1963–1969)

The Civil Rights Act is passed, which prohibits discrimination based on color, race, national origin, religion, or sex. (1964)

The Ed Sullivan Show on television introduces the Beatles to America. (1964)

Lyndon Baines Johnson
(1963–1969)

Soviet leader Nikita Khrushchev is ousted from power and is replaced by Leonid Brezhnev. (1964)

Civil-rights leader Martin Luther King, Jr., and Senator Robert F. Kennedy are assassinated. (1968)

During the Presidency of Richard Milhous Nixon (1969–1974)

American astronaut Neil Armstrong is the first man to walk on the moon, saying: "That's one small step for a man, one giant leap for mankind." (1969)

The Woodstock Music Festival is held in upstate New York. (1969)

National guardsmen kill four students at Kent State University in Ohio during an antiwar protest. (1970)

The Twenty-sixth Amendment to the Constitution lowers the voting age to 18. (1971)

Diplomatic relations are resumed with Communist China after Nixon visits that country. (1972)

Arab terrorists kill 11 Israeli athletes at the Summer Olympics in Munich, Germany. (1972)

The so-called energy shortage triggers massive lines at gas stations across the country. (1973)

Daylight saving time is extended to 18 months, instead of the usual 6 months, in an effort to conserve energy. (1973)

The Watergate scandal forces Richard Nixon to be the first president to resign. (1974)

Richard Milhous Nixon
(1969–1974)

During the Presidency of Gerald R. Ford (1974–1977)

President Ford issues a pardon to Richard Nixon, angering many Americans who want the former president tried for his role in Watergate. (1974)

Newspaper heiress Patricia Hearst is kidnapped by the Symbionese Liberation Army.

The capital of South Vietnam, Saigon, falls to communist North Vietnam. The frenetic evacuation of Saigon is televised to millions. (1975)

The United States celebrates its bicentennial on July 4th. (1976)

Two U.S. spacecraft, the *Viking I* and *Viking II*, land on Mars and begin transmitting the first photographs of the planet's surface. (1976)

Gerald Rudolph Ford
(1974–1977)

During the Presidency of James Earl Carter, Jr. (1977–1981)

The series *Roots*, about the impact of slavery on generations of African-American families, gains the largest viewing audience in television history. (1977) The United States agrees to turn over control of the Panama Canal to the Panamanian government by the year 2000. (1978)

A near-accident at Three Mile Island in Pennsylvania raises safety concerns about nuclear power plants. (1979)

James Earl Carter, Jr.
(1977–1981)

Iranian militants take over the U.S. Embassy in Tehran, and 52 Americans are held captive for 444 days. (1979)

The Soviet Union invades Afghanistan. (1979)

The volcano Mount Saint Helens erupts in Washington State, killing 57 people. (1980)

During the Presidency of Ronald Reagan (1981–1989)

On the day of President Reagan's inauguration, Iranian militants release the 52 American hostages held for 444 days. (1981)

Sandra Day O'Connor becomes the first woman appointed to the position of Supreme Court justice. (1981)

The term *yuppie*, short for "young urban professional," is coined. It refers to

Ronald Wilson Reagan
(1981–1989)

upwardly mobile young adults in cities and suburbs. (1982)

A mysterious disease, later identified as autoimmune deficiency syndrome (AIDS), begins to appear in the nation's urban areas. (1983)

Wall Street becomes the place to be—fueled by a frenzy of investment-banking fortunes and the widening impact of computer technology. (1985)

The space shuttle *Challenger* explodes in midair, killing all seven people aboard, including high-school teacher Christa McAuliffe, who was specially selected as the first teacher-in-space to ride with the astronauts. (1986)

The nation celebrates the centennial of the erection of the Statue of Liberty. (1986)

Due to pressures within East Germany, the Berlin Wall, a symbol of the Cold War, falls. (1989)

During the Presidency of George H. W. Bush 1989–1993)

The supertanker *Exxon Valdez* spills 11 million gallons of crude oil off the Alaskan coast. It is the largest oil spill in history. (1989)

General Colin Powell becomes the first African-American to be appointed Chairman of the Joint Chiefs of Staff. (1989)

The Americans with Disabilities Act becomes law. (1990)

The European Space Agency (ESA) and the National Aeronautics and Space Administration (NASA) launch the Hubble Space Telescope. (1990)

George Herbert Walker Bush
(1989–1993)

Iraqi forces invade Kuwait, igniting the Persian Gulf War. (1991)

As the former Soviet Union begins to redefine itself, many of its former states begin to declare their independence. The city of Leningrad adopts its prerevolutionary name, St. Petersburg. (1991)

After a jury finds innocent three police officers accused of assaulting African-American motorist Rodney King, four days of rioting break out in Los Angeles. (1992)

The federal budget deficit stands at $290 billion, the largest dollar deficit in American history. (1992)

During the Presidency of William J. Clinton (1993–2001)

Civil war erupts in the former country of Yugoslavia, killing thousands of civilians in Bosnia, Serbia, Croatia, and other parts of the Balkan Peninsula. In

Kosovo, a reported estimate of 2,700 people died in 1998–1999. (1990s)

While on a peacekeeping mission, eight U.S. soldiers are shot down over Mogadishu, Somalia, and brutally murdered at the directive of warlord Mohammed Aidid. (1993)

A bomb explodes outside a government building in Oklahoma City, killing 168 people and injuring hundreds more. (1995)

Madeleine Albright is appointed U.S. Secretary of State; she is the first woman to hold that position. (1996)

Automakers manufacture successful, roadworthy electric vehicles in 1996. Oil companies

William Jefferson Clinton
(1993–2001)

reportedly buy up patents for greatly improved batteries as discussion of alternative fuels diverts public attention. Over 1,000 electric cars, recalled from satisfied drivers who leased them, are crushed at General Motors' Mesa, Arizona, proving grounds in 2003.

Scottish scientists introduce Dolly, the first successfully cloned sheep. (1997)

The spacecraft *Pathfinder* lands on Mars on July 4, 1997, and explores the red planet with a robotic roaming vehicle named *Sojourner*.

The Clinton Administration reduces the federal budget deficit, and the Office of Management and Budget projects a record surplus of at least $230 billion for 2000, even after adjusting for inflation.

Terrorists bomb the U.S. embassies in Kenya and Tanzania. (1998)

During the Presidency of George Walker Bush (2001–   )

Amid political and ethical debate, Bush vetoes use of federal funds for research on use of embryonic stem cells for treating and preventing disease. (2001)

On September 11, 2001, terrorists crash two hijacked airliners into New York's World Trade Center towers, which collapse. A third hijacked plane damages the Pentagon, and a fourth crashes in a Pennsylvania field. The combined death toll is nearly 3,000.

George Walker Bush
(2001–   )

On October 7, 2001, the United States and Great Britain begin military strikes in Afghanistan against Al Qaeda and the Taliban, while searching for terrorist leader Osama bin Ladin and others responsible for the September 11, 2001, attacks.

The space shuttle *Columbia* breaks up on reentry into the earth's atmosphere, killing the crew of seven astronauts. (2003)

On March 20, 2003, Bush declares war against Iraq, based on the belief that "weapons of mass destruction" exist within the country. By 2006, no such weapons are found.

The September 11 Commission reports that no "collaborative relationship" has been found between Iraq and Al Qaeda. (2004)

Hurricane Katrina causes devastation in Louisiana, Mississippi, and Alabama. Six months after the storm, over 1,600 are confirmed dead, and over 1,800 others are reported as still missing. Federal rescue efforts are criticized as disorganized and incompetent. (2005)

Bush introduces legislation to privatize Social Security and dismantle the social welfare system introduced by Franklin D. Roosevelt and expanded by Lyndon B. Johnson. (2005)

The National Academy of Sciences cites greenhouse gases, burning fossil fuels, and human activity as major causes of climate change. (2005)

With the war in Iraq costing $5 billion a month, the federal deficit reaches over $1 trillion. This does not include the estimated $200 billion required to rebuild Katrina-ravaged New Orleans. (2006)

British and Pakistani authorities thwart a terrorist plot to destroy ten planes bound for the U.S. with liquid bombs disguised as sports drinks and other liquids or gels packed in carry-on bags. (2006)

A U.S. District Court judge in Detroit rules that the National Security Agency's wiretapping on American citizens without a warrant is unconstitutional. (2006)

Pluto loses its status as a planet. (2006)

Chapter 2
Presidential Firsts, Lasts, and Onlys

For the most part, American presidents stand out for their accomplishments. But some might be better remembered for what they looked like, what they wore, what they ate, who they married, and other curious details—many of which were shrouded in secrecy until their terms of office were comfortably finished. Here is just a sampling.

Oldest and Youngest, Tallest and Shortest

Of all the U.S. presidents, the second president, John Adams lived to be the second oldest. When he died in 1801, he was 90 years and 247 days old; he had been ex-president for 25 years and 4 months—longer than any other ex-president. Ronald Reagan was the oldest American president; he was elected at age 69 and died at 93.

The youngest man to become president was Teddy Roosevelt at age 42 in 1901. He was not elected president, but succeeded President William McKinley, who had been assassinated.

The youngest elected president was John F. Kennedy at age 43 in 1961.

Abraham Lincoln was 6 feet 4 inches tall, the tallest president so far.

James Madison stood 5 feet 4 inches, the shortest president.

Presidential Terms

Grover Cleveland (1885–1889, 1893–1897) was elected president in 1884, voted out of office in 1888, and voted back in 1892. This makes him the only president to serve two nonconsecutive terms in office. He was also the only Democratic president between 1869 and 1913.

Franklin D. Roosevelt was the only president elected to four terms. He completed the first three terms, but died during his fourth term. He was first elected president in 1932, and elected again in 1936, 1940, and 1944.

Presidents' Families

John Tyler had fifteen children; his was the largest family of any president.

Thomas Jefferson was the first president to have a grandchild born in the White House.

John Quincy Adams was the first and only president to name a son George Washington.

In 1893 Grover Cleveland became the first president to have a child, Esther (his second child), born in the White House.

The only presidents whose fathers were also presidents were John Quincy Adams, the sixth, and George W. Bush, the 43rd president.

Modern Conveniences

In 1833 Andrew Jackson was the first president to have running water piped into the White House, and in 1853 Franklin Pierce had an efficient hot-water heating system installed in the White House.

In 1835 the first central heating system was installed in the White House.

Millard Fillmore in the 1850s was reportedly the first president to have a stove in the White House.

In 1877, Rutherford B. Hayes was the first president to use a telephone while in office; the White House phone number was "1."

Benjamin Harrison in 1891 was the first president to use electricity in the White House and to sign his papers under an electric light.

Elections

Under the First Continental Congress, Peyton Randolph was elected as its first president. John Hancock was the most famous of these early presidents, having presided during the Declaration of Independence. Note that the office of the president of the Continental Congress (a legislative body) had little in common with what later became the office of the president of the United States (an executive body).

George Washington was the only president elected unanimously, receiving all 69 of the electoral votes cast.

John Tyler (1841–1845) was playing marbles when he learned that he would become president.

James K. Polk was the first president elected to serve

the continental U.S., once it expanded to the West Coast.

President Zachary Taylor never voted for a president himself.

Millard Fillmore was the last sitting president to be denied nomination for a second term by his political party. He lost the Whig Party nomination to Winfield Scott in 1852.

In 1880, James Garfield (1881) became the first presidential candidate to spend more than $1 million on his campaign. He was also elected to the presidency while serving in the House of Representatives.

Harry S. Truman was playing poker when he found out that he would become president.

Before he was elected president, Dwight D. Eisenhower never voted.

John F. Kennedy was the last person to be elected directly from the Senate to the presidency.

Gerald Ford was the only president not elected as president or vice president. He was appointed vice president by President Richard Nixon and then became president when Richard Nixon resigned in 1973. Very attractive and athletic as a young man, Ford had been a model for *Cosmopolitan* and *Look* magazines in the 1940s.

Inaugurations

George Washington became president on April 30, 1789, in New York City.

Andrew Johnson was the only vice president to be drunk at his inauguration in 1865. He was ill and had taken brandy to "fortify himself."

Presidential Appointments

The youngest federal judge ever was Thomas Jefferson Boynton, who was 25 when Abraham Lincoln issued him a recess appointment to the

U.S. District Court for the Southern District of Florida on October 19, 1863.

In 1933 Franklin D. Roosevelt appointed Frances Perkins as the first female cabinet member in U.S. history. She was appointed Secretary of Labor and served for twelve years, from 1933 to 1945.

Franklin D. Roosevelt in 1934 appointed Florence Allen as the first woman to serve on the U.S. Circuit Court of Appeals. She served the Sixth Circuit.

John F. Kennedy appointed Reynaldo G. Garza, the first Hispanic federal court judge, to the U.S. District Court for the Southern District of Texas in 1961. Garza later became the first Hispanic judge on a U.S. Court of Appeals when President Jimmy Carter appointed him to the Fifth Circuit Court of Appeals in 1979.

In 1967 Lyndon B. Johnson appointed Thurgood Marshall to the U.S. Supreme Court. Justice Marshall was the first African-American to serve on the Supreme Court. In 1991 George H. W. Bush appointed

Clarence Thomas, the second African-American to serve as Supreme Court justice.

In 1981, Ronald Reagan appointed Sandra Day O'Connor to the U.S. Supreme Court. O'Connor, a former assistant attorney general, state senator, and appeals court judge in Arizona, became the first woman to serve on the Supreme Court.

In 1993 Bill Clinton appointed Ruth Bader Ginsburg to the Supreme Court. She was the second woman to serve on the high court.

Manners, Fashion, and Appearances

George Washington was the first president to appear on a postage stamp.

Thomas Jefferson was the first president to greet guests by shaking hands instead of bowing.

James Madison was the first president to wear trousers rather than knee breeches.

Abraham Lincoln was the first president to wear a beard while in office.

William Howard Taft was the first president to throw out the first baseball of the major league season. Walter Johnson caught the ball Taft pitched.

John Quincy Adams in 1843 was the first president to be photographed. (He was not president at the time the photograph was taken.) Six years later, President James Polk was the first president to be photographed while in office.

They Also Served

Washington was the first man in U.S. history to be a lieutenant general.

James Madison was the first president with prior service as a congressman. As a Virginia representative, Madison served from 1789 to 1797.

William Howard Taft was the only ex-president to be appointed as chief justice of the Supreme Court.

President Warren G. Harding appointed him in 1921.

Scholars

Woodrow Wilson was the only president with a Ph.D. He earned his doctorate in political science from Johns Hopkins University in 1885 and became president of Princeton University in 1902.

Bill Clinton was the first president to have been a Rhodes Scholar (1968), which allowed him to study at Oxford University.

Births and Deaths

Martin Van Buren was the first president to be born a U.S. citizen. The presidents who preceded him had been born in one of the original Thirteen Colonies, which had been part of the British Empire.

Herbert Hoover was the first president born west of the Mississippi River. He was born on August 10, 1874, in West Branch, Iowa.

Jimmy Carter was the first president born in a hospital. He was born on October 1, 1924.

Washington was the only president to die in the 1700s.

William Henry Harrison (1841) was the first president to die while in office.

Presidents Kennedy and Taft are the only presidents buried in Arlington National Cemetery.

Presidential Travels

Andrew Jackson was the first president to ride a train.

Ulysses S. Grant was the first and only president to get a speeding ticket while in office. He was driving a horse and buggy; the fine was $20.

Teddy Roosevelt was the first president to travel outside the country while in office. In 1906, he went to Panama to review progress on the construction of the Panama Canal.

Franklin D. Roosevelt became the first president to travel through the Panama Canal.

Teddy Roosevelt was the first president to ride in a car while in office. He rode in a brand new 1903 Columbia Electric in the fall of 1902.

Teddy Roosevelt was the first ex-president to fly in an airplane. Archibald Hoxsey piloted the Wright model B plane with Roosevelt on board in 1910.

In June 1943 Franklin D. Roosevelt became the first president to visit a foreign country during wartime.

In 1943 Franklin D. Roosevelt, however, was the first president to fly in a plane *while* he was president. He was also the first president to own his own plane.

Teddy Roosevelt in 1905 on Long Island Sound, boarded the Plunger, a submarine that reached a depth of 40 feet below the water's surface and rested motionless as a storm raged above.

Harry S. Truman was the first president to travel in a modern submarine in Key West, Florida, in 1946.

Flight

Both George Washington and Thomas Jefferson witnessed the first successful flight of a human being in North America on January 9, 1793. The French argonaut Jean Pierre Blanchard conducted a balloon flight that started in Philadelphia.

Eisenhower was the first president to obtain a private pilot's license (1939), fly in a helicopter (1957), and fly in a jet-powered aircraft. He learned to fly while serving on General Douglas MacArthur's staff in the Philippines.

George H. W. Bush was the first president to be a four-time survivor. He survived four plane crashes while serving in World War II.

George W. Bush's pilot's license was reportedly revoked in 1978 because he did not appear for a physical.

The Press

John Adams ordered his Attorney General to prosecute William Duane, an opposition newspaper editor, under the infamous Sedition Act.

James Knox Polk was the first president to have his inauguration (1845) reported by telegraph.

Warren G. Harding was the first president to speak on the radio.

Teddy Roosevelt was the first president to establish the White House Press Room. Roosevelt reportedly felt sorry for the reporters standing out in the rain in front of the White House.

Woodrow Wilson was the first president to hold a press conference.

Herbert Hoover spoke and was pictured on the first transmission of television signals from New York to Washington in 1927. This occurred before he became president.

In 1939 Franklin D. Roosevelt was the first to appear on television while serving as president.

Franklin D. Roosevelt invented a Dunce Cap Club, to which he would banish reporters whose questions annoyed him during press conferences.

To make room for more reporters, Harry S. Truman moved the press conferences from the Oval Office to the Indian Treaty Room in the Executive Office Building.

Dwight D. Eisenhower held the first tape-recorded news conference on December 16, 1953. He also held the first filmed news conference on January 19, 1955.

John F. Kennedy was the first president to hold a live televised news conference on January 25, 1961.

Richard Nixon covered over the White House swimming pool to create new luxurious quarters for the press corps. Later, President Ford had another pool dug on the White House lawn.

The Nixon Administration was the first to succeed temporarily in preventing the press from publishing some information it found objectionable. For fifteen days in 1971, until the Supreme Court acted, a federal court order prevented the *New York Times* from publishing the *Pentagon Papers*.

In Moscow, Richard Nixon's speech was broadcast from the Kremlin on television and radio in the Soviet Union on May 28, 1972. He was the first president to address the Soviets on Soviet television.

The Supreme Court

George Washington was the first and only president to nominate all members of the Supreme Court.

William Howard Taft was the first and only president to become the chief justice of the United States Supreme Court.

Woodrow Wilson was the first president to appoint a Jewish Supreme Court Justice—Louis D. Brandeis.

Jimmy Carter was the only full-term president who did not appoint anyone to the Supreme Court.

John F. Kennedy nominated Byron White, a former National Football League rookie of the year, to the Supreme Court. It was the first nomination of a sports figure for this post.

Warren Burger was the first justice of the Supreme Court to be summoned from overseas to conduct a swearing-in of a new president. The president was Gerald Ford after the resignation of Richard Nixon. *Air Force One* was dispatched to pick up Justice Burger and his wife.

Civil Rights

On June 24, 1941, Franklin D. Roosevelt issued an executive order banning racial discrimination in government employment, defense industries, and training programs—the first executive order of its kind. Roosevelt also established the Fair Employment Practices Committee (FEPC) to enforce this order.

Harry S. Truman ended racial discrimination in the military in 1948. The same year, Truman also issued an executive order banning racial discrimination in federal employment.

Self-Expression

Teddy Roosevelt wasn't the only president to invent a new expression ("bully for you"). Martin Van Buren is sometimes credited with creating the word *O.K.* Van Buren was from Kinderhook, New York. During his 1836 campaign for president, Old Kinderhook (O.K.) clubs formed to support the president. Later, the term OK (also spelled *okay*) came to mean "all correct" (or facetiously, "oll korrect").

George H. W. Bush was the first president to publicly refuse to eat broccoli.

Bill Clinton played the saxophone on national television; he appeared on *The Tonight Show* with Johnny Carson before he became president.

Presidents and Their Wives

The term *First Lady* originated with Martha Washington. Very much under the influence of British etiquette, the Washington press called Martha Washington "Lady Washington." But Martha preferred First Lady, which continues today.

James Buchanan was the only president never to marry. Five presidents remarried after the death of their first wives—two of whom, Tyler and Wilson—remarried while in the White House. Reagan was the only divorced president. Six presidents had no children. Tyler, father of fifteen, had the most.

John Adams was married longer than any other president. His marriage to Abigail Smith Adams lasted 54 years and 3 months.

Grover Cleveland was the only president to be married in the White House. The wedding was in 1886.

The White House

The nation's capital was located in New York and Philadelphia during Washington's administration, making him the only president who did not live in Washington, D.C., or the White House during his presidency.

The site for the White House was chosen along the Potomac in 1790.

John Adams (1797–1801) was the first president to live in the White House. He and his wife Abigail moved into the house in 1800.

In 1809 the first heating system, a gravity-based Pettibone furnace, was installed in the White House when James Monroe took office.

In the War of 1812 with the British, the Capitol and White House were burned in 1814. It was reconstructed, and James Monroe moved into the building still under construction in 1817.

James Monroe was the first president whose daughter, Maria, married in the White House. Maria Monroe married Samuel Gouverneur, March 9, 1820.

In 1850 Millard Fillmore became the first president to establish a permanent library in the White House.

Franklin Pierce was the first president to have a Christmas tree in the White House. In 1856, the tree was set up for a group of Sunday-school children from Washington, D.C.

When William McKinley was president, the White House grounds were open to the public and used by everyone like a park. On warm evenings, McKinley often sat under the south portico to dine, sometimes even chatting with curious onlookers.

It was Teddy Roosevelt who officially named the executive mansion the White House by presidential proclamation in 1901.

In 1922 Warren G. Harding had a radio installed in a bookcase in his study, and in 1925 Calvin Coolidge made the first radio broadcast from the White House.

In 1923 President Calvin Coolidge lit the first Christmas tree on the White House lawn.

Other Deeds

Thomas Jefferson was the first president to cite the doctrine of executive privilege by refusing to testify at the treason trial of Aaron Burr.

Andrew Jackson was the only president to ever kill a man in a duel.

John Tyler was the first president to have a veto overridden.

Andrew Jackson was the first president to nearly pay off the national debt.

John F. Kennedy was the first president to have been a Boy Scout.

Dwight D. Eisenhower was the only president to have served in both World War I and World War II.

Chapter 3
Presidential Nicknames

Some nicknames compliment; others ridicule. George Washington, the "Sword of the Revolution," was followed by "His Rotundity," John Adams. Thomas Jefferson, the "Sage of Monticello," was followed by "The Short Sir," James Madison. One thing seems certain—the more modern the president, the harsher the nickname. Can anyone deny that "Tricky Dick" will always be associated with Richard Nixon? Politicians beware!

White House staffers, if we are to believe television shows, refer to their boss as POTUS, or Potus, which stands for the "President of the United States."

George Washington

- The Father of His Country
- The Sword of the Revolution
- The Gentleman of Mount Vernon
- The Gentleman Farmer
- His High Duty *Washington refused to accept a salary while serving as president.*
- The American Fabius *This was an accolade for Washington's military strategies during the Revolutionary War.*
- Town Destroyer *coined by the Iroquois*

John Adams

- Atlas of Independence
- Old Sink or Swim
- The President Scholar *The Library of Congress was established while Adams was in office.*
- His Rotundity *They noted his girth.*
- The Pilgrim President *He was a direct descendant of John and Priscilla Alden of the Mayflower.*

Thomas Jefferson

- Father of the Declaration of Independence
- Pen of the Revolution
- The Sage of Monticello *His home was in Monticello, Virginia.*
- Philosopher Thomas
- Fiddlin' Thomas *Jefferson was an accomplished musician.*
- Thomas French *His previous career was as minister to France.*
- The Louisiana Purchaser *He doubled the size of the United States through the Louisiana Purchase.*

James Madison

- Father of the Constitution
- Father of the Bill of Rights
- President Long Pants *Madison was the first president to wear long pants instead of knee breeches.*

- The Short Sir *Madison was only 5 feet, 4 inches tall, the shortest president up to that time.*
- No-Heirs Madison *James and Dolley Madison never had children.*
- Withered Little Apple-John *Writer Washington Irving called him this.*

James Monroe
- Last of the Cocked Hats *Soldiers of the American Revolution wore three-corner hats. Monroe was the last president from this era.*
- Musical Monroe *At his second inauguration, held outdoors, Monroe began the tradition of having the Marine Band play.*
- Protector of the Territories *The Monroe Doctrine prohibited European countries from interfering in the affairs of the countries of North and South America.*
- President Good Feeling *Political bickering that characterized his first term.*

John Quincy Adams
- Old Man Eloquent *His speeches were long and articulate.*

- King John II *He was the second "John Adams"; his father served as president after Washington.*
- The Abolitionist *As a member of the House of Representative, he voiced his strong opposition to slavery.*

Andrew Jackson
- Old Hickory and Hero of New Orleans *Both refer to his leadership during the War of 1812.*
- President of the Common Man *He was born in a log cabin.*
- The Orphan President *An orphan by the age of 13, he took up arms in the Revolutionary War.*
- King Andy

Martin Van Buren
- Machiavellian Belshazzar *He was considered a conniving campaigner.*
- Petticoat Pet *He was supposedly henpecked.*
- Old Kinderhook *His birthplace was Kinderhook, New York. Supporters of Van Buren formed the OK Club, which some say accounts for the origin of the term OK.*

- Old Bungler *He inherited serious economic problems from his predecessor, Andrew Jackson.*
- Little Magician *He was a shrewd political operator.*
- Red Fox of Kinderhook and The Sage of Lindenwald *He had homes in the upstate New York towns of Kinderhook and Lindenwald*

William Henry Harrison

- Tippecanoe and Savior of Indiana *This refers to his victory over Native Americans in the Battle of Tippecanoe. The campaign slogan was "Tippecanoe and Tyler, too." Tyler was his vice-presidential running mate.*
- The Old Man *He took office at age 69.*
- Granny Harrison *This was derived from a political cartoon.*
- Short-Term Harrison *He died after only 32 days in office.*

John Tyler

- His Accidency *Tyler received the job because Harrison died in office.*

- Secession John *He supported the secession of the slave-holding states from the Union.*
- Savior of Maine *He settled an important boundary dispute with the Seminoles.*

James K. Polk
- Young Hickory *He was backed by Old Hickory, Andrew Jackson.*
- Napoleon of the Stump *He gave fiery speeches.*
- President and Mrs. Church *Sarah Polk did not allow dancing, card playing, or liquor in the White House.*
- Conqueror of Mexico *The U.S. victory in the Mexican–American War added a vast amount of land to the country.*

Zachary Taylor
- Old Rough and Ready *He was a hero of the Mexican–American War.*
- Old Zachy
- Honest Zach
- President Stable *His horse, Whitey, was stabled on the White House lawn.*

Millard Fillmore

- **The Bookworm** *He constructed the first library in the White House.*
- **Gentleman Lawyer**
- **Fugitive Fillmore and President Bounty Hunter** *He signed an unpopular "Fugitive Slave Act," requiring runaway slaves to be returned to their owners.*
- **The American Louis Philippe** *This was an unflattering comparison with the contemporary King of France who allied himself with the ruling class.*
- **The Accidental President** *His predecessor, Zachary Taylor, died in office.*
- **Wool-Carder President** *He had been an apprentice to a wool carder.*

Franklin Pierce

- **Young Hickory of Granite Hills** *This referred to his home.*
- **The Great Rememberer** *He recited his inaugural address completely from memory.*

- The Bungler of Kansas *He mishandled a revolt concerning slavery in the Kansas territory.*
- Handsome Frank

James Buchanan
- The Bachelor President *Buchanan was the only unmarried president; his niece served as First Lady.*
- Ten-Cent Jimmy *He once claimed that 10 cents a day was enough pocket money for any man.*
- Ten-Cents-a-Day Jimmy
- Old Public Functionary *This refers to one of his State of the Union Addresses.*
- Old Buck
- The Sage of Wheatland *Wheatland was his home in Pennsylvania.*
- The Russian *He served as minister to Russia under Andrew Jackson.*
- The Great Compromiser *He advocated the right to own slaves but was against secession.*

Abraham Lincoln
- The Great Emancipator *He signed and ratified the Emancipation Proclamation.*

- Black Republican
- Honest Abe
- The Log-Splitter and The Rail-Splitter *These allude to his former occupation.*

- The Sectional President *The country was divided during his term.*
- The Sage of Springfield *Springfield, Illinois, had been his hometown.*
- The Martyr *He was assassinated.*

Andrew Johnson
- Father of the Homestead Act
- Tennessee Tailor *His home state was Tennessee and he had been a tailor.*
- Sir Veto *He vetoed many bills that would have protected freed slaves.*

Ulysses Simpson Grant
- Hero of Appomattox *This refers to his military service.*
- Unconditional Surrender Grant *This plays on his initials and his terms for enemy surrender during the Civil War.*

- Useless Grant *This pejorative nickname came from people in the former Confederate states.*

Rutherford Birchard Hayes
- The Dark Horse President *No one expected him to win.*
- Rutherfraud, His Fraudulency, and Old Eight to Seven *Democrat Samuel Tilden won the popular vote but not the electoral vote. Popular opinion held that Republicans had rigged the election.*

James Abram Garfield
- The Preacher President *He was once a preacher.*
- Boatman Jim and Canal Boy *During the American Civil War, he won battles in Kentucky near Jenny's Creek and Middle Creek.*

Chester Alan Arthur
- The Dude President *This reflects on his manner of dress.*
- The Gentleman Boss
- Elegant Arthur

(Stephen) Grover Cleveland

- The Hangman of Buffalo *His former career was as a sheriff and sometime executioner in Buffalo, New York.*
- The Veto President *He vetoed many spending bills.*
- Uncle Jumbo *His body was large.*
- Big Steve *While commonly known only as Grover Cleveland, his real first name was Stephen.*

Benjamin Harrison

- The Whitehouse Iceberg *His hair was as pure white as his beard.*
- Kid Gloves Harrison *There was a Democratic party mudslinging campaign against him.*
- Grandfather's Hat

William McKinley

- The Idol of Ohio *His roots were in Ohio.*
- Stocking-Footed Orator *He often gave impromptu directions to staff in his stocking feet.*
- Wobbly Willie

Theodore Roosevelt

- Teddy
- TR
- Great White Chief
- The Elephant Rider
  He loved African safaris.
- Trustbuster
- The Cyclone Assemblyman
- The Victor of Cuba *He was in command of the Rough Riders, a special fighting force that invaded Cuba in 1898.*
- The Peacemaker *He successfully mediated the Russo–Japanese War and was awarded the Nobel Peace Prize.*
- Rough Rider, The Hero of San Juan Hill, and That Damned Cowboy *This reflects on his part in the Spanish–American War and membership in the cavalry unit, the Rough Riders.*

William Howard Taft

- Big Bill *He weighed over 300 pounds.*
- Bill Dollar *He used "dollar diplomacy" and*

occasionally used force to promote U.S. business around the world.

- President Do Nothing *He didn't believe in an active presidency.*

(Thomas) Woodrow Wilson

- Schoolmaster in Politics *He was the former president of Princeton University.*
- The Schoolmaster
- The Phrase-Maker and Coiner of Weasel Words
- President Spectacles

Warren Gamaliel Harding

- President Hardly *Many believed that Harding hardly made any impact during his administration.*
- The Corruptor *His administration was widely considered the most corrupt since the Grant Administration.*
- The Poker President *Harding was reputed to have held poker and drinking parties during Prohibition.*

(John) Calvin Coolidge

- Silent Cal *He was shy and a poor public speaker.*

- Tired Cal *He had been woken up to take the oath of office after Harding's death and then went back to sleep.*
- President Business *He believed government should not interfere with business.*

Herbert Clark Hoover
- Hermit Author of Palo Alto
- The Great Humanitarian *He's credited with saving millions of Europeans from destitution after World War I due to his skillful distribution of aid.*
- The Great Engineer
- President Hooverville *Shanty dwellings were common during the Great Depression.*

Franklin Delano Roosevelt
- Fearless FDR *In his famous speech broadcast on radio, he announced, ""We have nothing to fear but fear itself."*
- The Sphinx
- That Man in the White House
- Unstoppable Franklin *He served for four consecutive terms.*

- The Voice
- The Friend of the Common People
- President Protector of the People
- The Socialist President
- One of a Pair *His wife, Eleanor Roosevelt, took an active role in national politics and world affairs.*
- The New Dealer and a Traitor to His Class *These refer to his New Deal policy. Roosevelt came from the upper class.*

Harry S. Truman

- Give 'Em Hell Harry
- T.V. Harry *His inauguration was the first to be televised.*
- Old Man Harry *Truman was the oldest man to take over the presidency upon a president's eath.*
- Haberdasher Harry *His previous occupation was as a haberdasher.*
- The Bomb Diplomat *In World War II, he allowed the atomic bombing of Hiroshima and Nagasaki, Japan.*

Dwight David Eisenhower

- Ike
- Baby Face
- Mr. Five-Star *He was a five-star general when he ran for president.*
- General President
- The Protector *He sent troops to Little Rock, Arkansas, to enforce a Supreme Court order ending segregation.*

John Fitzgerald Kennedy

- JFK
- Jack
- King of Camelot *Perceived to be cultured and enlightened, Kennedy fostered these qualities in his administration.*
- Dashing John *He was considered good-looking, although the Irish name Kennedy means "ugly head."*
- Jackie Kennedy's husband
- Pedigree Kennedy
- High Talker
- The Joker

- The Cuba Hero *When the Soviet Union threatened to place missiles, pointed at the U.S., on Cuban soil, Kennedy took action.*
- Football John
- Choirboy Kennedy *He had an Irish Catholic background.*

Lyndon Baines Johnson
- LBJ
- Landslide Lyndon
- Old Barbecue
- Ear Grabber *He grabbed the ears of a dog in a photograph.*
- Down Homer
- Friend-to-Anybody

Richard Milhous Nixon
- Gloomy Gus *His nickname while in law school.*
- Tricky Dick
- The Lottery President *He implemented the lottery to replace the draft.*
- Mill House *His middle name was Milhous.*
- President Watergate

- The Deceiver *Sections of taped conversations, that could be evidence in the Watergate investigation, were mysteriously erased.*
- Dick Quitter
- Nix-On-Dick

Gerald Rudolph Ford
- Jerry
- Mr. Nice Guy
- Mr. Bicentennial
- Betty's Husband *His popularity took a second seat to that of his wife, Betty Ford.*
- Fall-Down Gerry *When getting off a plane, he fell down steps. Although he had been an athlete, his supposed physical awkwardness was noted.*
- Dicky's Angel *He pardoned Richard Nixon for his part in the Watergate scandal.*

James Earl Carter, Jr.
- Jimmy Carter
- Jimmy Peanut *The Carter family owned peanut farms in Georgia.*
- Peanut Farmer

- President Squeak *His high voice sounded squeaky on occasion.*
- Jimmy Nose
- Square Dancer
- Lillian's Boy *He made frequent appearances with Lillian Carter, his mother.*

Ronald Wilson Reagan
- The Gipper *In his movie career, he played the football hero George "the Gipper" Gipp in the film* Knute Rockne, All American, *where he said, "Win this one for the Gipper."*
- The Great Communicator *Although not considered a deep thinker, his fine oratory and written skills won praise.*
- The Teflon President *He was able to dodge blame during political scandals.*
- Ronnie Raygun *He used a* Star Wars *analogy when projecting his national defense-system ideas.*
- Dutch
- Rawhide *This was his Secret Service code name.*
- President Nap *He was reputed to doze off during staff meetings.*

- The Feel Good President
- The Greed-Is-Good President
- Nancy's Patsy *Many people suggested that his wife Nancy was the real power behind the president.*
- The Great Prevaricator
- President Say Nothing *He refused to speak about AIDS.*
- President No Comment *He curtailed information to the press.*
- Contra Ronnie *This refers to his ill-conceived plan to aid the Contra insurgency in Nicaragua.*

George Herbert Walker Bush

- Bush 41 *George H. W. Bush was the 41st president.*
- Bush the Elder
- Daddy Bush
- Poppy
- Mr. Résumé *He served in the House of Representatives and was appointed as ambassador to the United Nations, director of the C.I.A., and chairman of the Republican National Committee, among other posts.*
- Fire-Bomber of Baghdad
- Goon of the Gulf War
- President Nothing

William Jefferson Clinton

- Bill Clinton
- Slick Willie
- Bubba
- Big Dog
- Comeback Kid *In spite of conservatives' many attempts to implicate him in scandals, the public loved him.*
- The first Black president *Writing in* The New Yorker, *Toni Morrison coined this term.*

George Walker Bush

- GWB
- Bush 43 *He was the 43rd president.*
- Baby Bush
- Shrub *Political satirist Molly Ivins referred to him as such in her syndicated newspaper column and in her book* Shrub: The Short but Happy Life of George W. Bush.
- Uncurious George
- The Smirking Chimp
- The Great Divider
- President Hilarity

- Resident Bush *His 2000 election was fraught with controversy about vote counting in Florida. The U.S. Supreme Court rather than the electorate decided the outcome. So the usual title of* president *became in popular thinking* resident.
- Dubya *For his middle initial ("W."), spoken with a Texas twang.*
- King George III *Maureen Dowd dubbed him this when he first took office. The nickname alludes to the monarch the Thirteen Colonies rebelled against during the American Revolution.*

Chapter 4
Presidents and Their Money

The commanders-in-chief have always been a bit secretive about their fortunes. And for good reason. "Money talks," as they say, and so do family connections. Most presidents came from politically well-connected backgrounds which prepared, if not financed, a rise to the very top. The few exceptions—Richard Nixon and Bill Clinton, to name an unlikely pair—were exceptional men of rare political talent and ambition. When self-made presidents displayed their wealth, Americans, for the most part, loved it.

   To the best of our knowledge and resources, these figures are accurate. Some may represent historical hearsay.

In matters of money, it's difficult to pin down exact figures regarding presidential wallets, bank accounts, stocks, land values, and spending habits.

John F. Kennedy's father gave him $1 million when he turned twenty-one. His father gave each of his ten children $1 million as well.

Ulysses S. Grant was arrested for speeding while driving a horse-drawn carriage in Washington, D.C. He had to pay a fine of $20 and walk back to the White House.

Warren G. Harding, while gambling, once lost all the chinaware that belonged to the White House.

Chester A. Arthur sold twenty-six wagons full of White House furniture for about $8,000. What he did not know was that the furniture was priceless. The money probably went toward buying new pants to add to Arthur's collection of eighty pairs. President Arthur felt the need to change pants several times a day.

Teddy Roosevelt unsuccessfully tried to have "In God We Trust" removed from all U.S. currency.

The portraits of Presidents Lincoln, Jefferson, Franklin D. Roosevelt, Washington, Kennedy, and Eisenhower appear on U.S. coins. The portraits of Presidents Washington, Jefferson, Lincoln, Jackson, Grant, McKinley, Cleveland, Madison, and Wilson appear on U.S. paper currency—various denominations of dollar bills.

Congress determines the salaries of its own members as well as that of the president.
    Congress offered George Washington an annual salary of $25,000, which he at first refused, reportedly favoring an expense account. He later changed his mind since he thought refusing a salary would establish a bad precedent.

George W. Bush's annual salary, established in January 1, 2001, was $400,000 plus a $50,000 annual expense allowance.

Often depicted wearing a tall black stovepipe hat, President Abraham Lincoln carried letters, bills, and notes in his hat.

"Wealth can only be accumulated by the earnings of industry and the savings of frugality."—John Tyler (1841)

"Whoever controls the volume of money in any country is absolute master of all industry and commerce."—James Garfield (1881)

"I sincerely believe...that banking establishments are more dangerous than standing armies, and that the principle of spending money to be paid by posterity under the name of funding is but swindling futurity on a large scale."—Thomas Jefferson to John Tyler (1816)

"When I was young, poverty was so common that we didn't know it had a name."—Lyndon B. Johnson

"Never fear the want of business. A man who qualifies himself well for his calling never fails of employment."—Thomas Jefferson

"Never spend your money before you have it."
—Thomas Jefferson

"I have the consolation of having added nothing to my private fortune during my public service, and of retiring with hands clean, as they are empty."
—Thomas Jefferson, 1807 letter to Count Diodati

As young men, both Abraham Lincoln and Harry S. Truman owned businesses that failed. Lincoln's failed general store left him with a huge debt that took several years to repay. Truman's haberdashery business failed in 1922 as a result of a recession. Truman repaid the debt over a period of fifteen years.

George Washington came from a wealthy planter family and became even wealthier when he married the widow Martha Dandridge Custis, the wealthiest woman in the colony of Virginia. Counting his Virginia plantation and his wife's fortune, Washington was one of the richest people of his day.

Washington spent more on housing and entertainment than his $25,000 presidential salary allowed.

On his death, in 1799, Washington's estate was valued in excess of $500,000. His main plantation at Mount Vernon had 300 slaves. Half belonged to Washington, and they were freed upon his death.

Jefferson owed more than $40,000 at his death, even after the sale of his properties, including the Monticello plantation.

Monroe left no estate at all, and William Henry Harrison was in debt.

Grant left no money. Only the manuscript of his memoirs kept his widow from being penniless.

The people of his time thought of Andrew Jackson (Old Hickory) as a commoner and backwoodsman. In fact, Andrew Jackson was one of the richest presidents of the 19th century. Jackson was raised by a well-off uncle before becoming a lawyer and earning a large fortune in real estate. However, when he left office, Andrew Jackson had only $90 in cash.

Andrew Jackson made his fortune while a general in the U.S. Army, taking land away from Native Americans. He and his army buddies developed and later sold those lands. Even people close to Jackson thought this practice was unfair. Jackson added to his fortunes by marrying the wealthy Rachel Donelson. He also owned a racetrack and was a successful gambler.

President Zachary Taylor's wealth came from inherited plantations. As descendants from *Mayflower* pilgrims, his family became major plantation owners in Mississippi, Louisiana, and Kentucky.

Adjusted for inflation and the economies of the day, William Howard Taft may have had the highest salary in constant dollars, making an amount close to $1.5 million in 2006 dollars.

   Nixon's salary would have bought what $1 million would today, and Washington's $25,000 salary of 1789 would be worth $500,000 today. By this measure, Clinton was the lowest paid president in American history.

Theodore Roosevelt's family was among the first settlers in New Amsterdam (present-day New York). His grandfather, Cornelius Van Schaack Roosevelt, was one of the wealthiest merchants and bankers in New York City during the mid-19th century.

Teddy Roosevelt enjoyed an inheritance providing him with an annual income of $8,000. In the mid-1800s to late 1800s, that was enough money to support a large home and servants, but not enough to run a townhouse in Manhattan. Teddy was much less well off than the rest of his family.

Before he was president, Teddy Roosevelt lost much of his fortune in an ill-fated ranching venture in the Dakota Territories.

After graduating from Stanford University, Herbert Hoover held a series of increasingly senior jobs with mining firms. His earnings and keen judgment allowed him to make successful investments in mining. By 1908, he was earning $100,000 per year.

When Herbert Hoover became president, he was worth more than $8 million—that's about $88 million in today's dollars. Hoover was one of the wealthiest presidents and probably the most successful businessman.

When John F. Kennedy was in power, his father, Joseph P. Kennedy, was worth up to $400 million, equal to about $2.6 billion in today's money. He gave John huge amounts of money. John's share of the Kennedy estate was worth $500,000 annually.

Kennedy was worth about $20 million when he was elected president, or $124 million in today's money. Kennedy received other benefits from his father, such as free use of the family yachts and access to grand properties on Cape Cod and in Florida.

President Lyndon B. Johnson's wealth came primarily from real estate and television and radio stations.

Johnson's father was a prosperous farmer, businessman, and state legislator who lost most of his fortune when the future president was 13. Johnson worked briefly as a school teacher, but entered politics at age 23. By the time he was president, he had a reported $14 million fortune.

Lyndon B. Johnson owed a great deal to his wife's good business sense. While Johnson was still a senator, his wife, *Lady Bird*, convinced him to purchase KTBC, a radio and television station in Austin, Texas. For a very long time this was the only television station in the Austin area. Some Texans believed that while a senator, Johnson pressured the Federal Communications Commission to keep KTBC's monopoly.

Lyndon B. Johnson was worth an estimated $14 million in 1966, *Life* magazine said at the time. That would be worth $82 million today. The magazine *Trusts and Estates* estimated Johnson's worth at $20 million in 1973, worth $85 million today.

Ronald Reagan was criticized for accepting $2 million to speak in Japan after his presidency.

Bill Clinton's 2005 book deal was reportedly worth $10 million. In signing the contract, Clinton took his place among the many former presidents who made up for their comparatively small salaries while in office.

President George W. Bush's disclosure statement indicates assets estimated at about $13 million. The value of the Bush family assets, managed by former President George H. W. Bush (father), remains a mystery.

When George H. W. Bush became vice president in 1980, his fortune was somewhere between $2 and $4 million. Upon entering the White House, George W. Bush, his son, was wealthier than his father due to the roughly $15 million he earned from the sale of his share of the Texas Rangers.

Senator John Kerry (who lost the 2004 presidential election) and his wife, Teresa Heinz Kerry, with assets of about $1 billion, would have been among the richest families to ever reside in the White House. They have even more money than the late John F. Kennedy.

A long list of presidents were helped by the wealth of their wives. George Washington, Thomas Jefferson, John Tyler, Lyndon B. Johnson, and William McKinley all married wealthy women.

While the dollar amount of presidential pay has increased steadily since George Washington's $25,000 salary, the actual spending power of presidents has dropped dramatically in recent decades due to inflation. Presidents today are actually paid less in real terms than earlier presidents. (Note inflation: $1 in 1750 equals about $154 today.)

Chester A. Arthur hired the famous glass designer Louis Comfort Tiffany to completely refurbish the White House. In fact, President Arthur loved luxury so much that the public nicknamed him "Gentleman Boss."

Grover Cleveland was the only president to have paid someone to substitute for him during the Civil War.

Penny Mystery

Why does the portrait of Abraham Lincoln on the penny face to the right when all other portraits of presidents on U.S. circulating coins face to the left? President Theodore Roosevelt was so impressed with a Lincoln plaque designed by Victor David Brenner, an outstanding portraitist and sculptor, that Roosevelt recommended that the design be placed as is—facing right, on a coin to be issued in 1909, the centennial year of Lincoln's birth.

The death of Franklin D. Roosevelt prompted many requests to the Treasury Department to honor the late president by placing his portrait on a coin. Less than one year after his death, the dime bearing John R. Sinnock's portrait of Franklin D. Roosevelt was released to the public in 1946, on FDR's birthday, January 30.

The portrait of George Washington by John Flanagan, which appears on quarters minted from 1932 to today, was selected to commemorate the 200th anniversary of our first president's birth.

The assassination of President John F. Kennedy generated such an outpouring of public sentiment that President Lyndon B. Johnson asked Congress to pass legislation authorizing the Treasury Department to mint new half-dollar pieces. Bearing the portrait designed by Gilroy Roberts, the first Kennedy half-dollars were minted on February 11, 1964.

The presidential portraits that today appear on the various denominations of paper currency were chosen by Congress, which held in 1929 that only portraits of U.S. presidents should appear on U.S. bills. But the Secretary of the Treasury petitioned Congress to include Benjamin Franklin and Alexander Hamilton, who was the first Secretary of the Treasury.

Which President on What Bill?

$1 Note
Face George Washington (1st U.S. president).
Back The Great Seal of the United States.

$2 Note*
Face Thomas Jefferson (3rd U.S. president).
Back Signing of the Declaration of Independence.

$5 Note
Face Abraham Lincoln (16th U.S. president).
Back Lincoln Memorial.

$10 Note
Face Alexander Hamilton (1st secretary of the Treasury).
Back U.S. Treasury Building.

$20 Note
Face Andrew Jackson (7th U.S. president).
Back White House.

$50 Note
Face Ulysses S. Grant (18th U.S. president).
Back U.S. Capitol.

$100 Note
Face Benjamin Franklin (statesman).
Back Independence Hall.

$500 Note*
Face William McKinley (25th U.S. president).
Back The numeral 500 and the words "Five Hundred Dollars."

$1,000 Note**
Face Grover Cleveland (22nd and 24th U.S. president).
Back The numeral 1,000 and the words "One Thousand Dollars."

$5,000 Note**
Face James Madison (4th U.S. president).
Back The numeral 5,000 and the words "Five Thousand Dollars."

$10,000 Note**
Face Salmon Chase (U.S. treasury secretary under Lincoln).
Back The numeral 10,000 and the words "Ten Thousand Dollars."

$100,000 Note**
Face Woodrow Wilson (28th U.S. president).
Back The numeral 100,000 and the words "One Hundred Thousand Dollars."

* Although the $2 bill is in circulation, relatively few people use them.

** The last distribution of the $500 bill was the 1934 series; however, there had been a previous printing in 1928, along with a more valuable gold certificate issue. The $1,000, $5,000, $10,000, and $100,000 bills never appeared in general circulation, and were only used in transactions between Federal Reserve banks.

National Debt

The federal government has been adding interest to its debt for 204 years. James Jackson, congressman from Georgia, predicted that this would happen in a speech he made to the nation's first Congress on February 9, 1790. Jackson warned that passing Alexander Hamilton's plan to base the country's money supply on the existing federal debt of $75 million would "settle upon our children a burden which they can neither bear nor relieve themselves from."

The federal debt was $75 million when Washington became president and $82 million when he left office. In 1836, Andrew Jackson had reduced the federal debt to $38,000, only to see the country plunge into a severe depression a year later.

The Cost of Being President

Today it takes a lot of money to win the presidency, but that wasn't always the case. George Washington spent almost nothing to become president. Neither did his five successors. In fact, up until William McKinley's time, presidential candidates had campaigns so small that they were able to handle the costs mostly out of their own pockets. McKinley was the first presidential candidate to actively solicit funds for his election. Appealing to wealthy friends and those who supported his platform, he quickly raised and spent over $7 million.

After his presidency, James Monroe lived with his daughter in New York. When he died in 1831, he was buried in New York rather than in his native Virginia because his family couldn't afford to ship his body back home.

After leaving the White House, President Truman and his wife, Bess, were forced to move into his mother-in-law's house in Independence, Missouri, due to lack of funds. Because of Truman's limited finances, Congress passed a law in 1958, called the Former Presidents Act. It provided a $25,000 annual pension to former presidents. In addition, former presidents and their families receive an expense account and additional perks.

They're entitled to fully paid staff as well as expenses covered for medical care, travel, office rental, telephone, postage, printing, and office supplies. Former presidents were also given round-the-clock protection from the Secret Service. The most expensive presidential perk is that of Secret Service protection. Today, the pension of a former president is about $167,000 a year.

It is difficult to determine the cost of air travel on *Air Force One*, partly because costs are confidential and spread over a number of agencies—the Departments of State and Defense, the Air Force, and the General Services Administration.

In 1990 the government purchased two new *Boeing 747–200Bs* for presidential use at a cost of approximately $650 million.

Taxpayers pay almost $1 billion to get their president airborne during his four years in office, not including the $6,000/hour fee to keep him aloft.

According to the *Los Angeles Times*, former President George H. W. Bush has been earning about $4 million annually delivering about 50 speeches a year.

Federal law does not limit how much money former presidents can earn, nor does it regulate how they go about earning it.

Richard Nixon was an expert poker player—despite the fact that his Quaker faith forbids gambling. He quickly became known as the best poker player in the Navy, having apparently won almost $10,000 by the end of World War II.

The annual budget for "the care, maintenance, repair

and alteration, refurnishing, improvement, heating, and lighting, including electric power and fixtures, of the Executive Residence at the White House and official entertainment expenses of the President," runs about $9 million dollars a year or about $25,000 a day. The cost of lawn and garden care around the White House is included in the $5 million budget spent annually to maintain the grounds of all the federal buildings in Washington, D.C.

Chapter 5
Presidents and Their Families

Presidents have their fair share of family embarrassments, and the whole world gets to watch. Scoundrels, criminals, difficult wives, outspoken brothers, and unruly children abound in even the most image-conscious administration, as poor President Franklin Roosevelt learned when asked to explain his wife Eleanor's interest in séances and the paranormal. George W. Bush also had some fast talking to do when quizzed about his daughters' behavior at a local watering spot. "They're just kids," he offered. Who could disagree?

Only three U.S. presidents married while they were in the White House. They were James Tyler, Grover Cleveland, and Woodrow Wilson.

James Buchanan was the only unmarried president. His fiancée committed suicide shortly before they were to be married, and her family would not allow Buchanan to attend her funeral.

John Quincy Adams and George W. Bush were the only presidents whose fathers were also presidents.

William Henry Harrison was the grandfather of Benjamin Harrison.

Franklin Roosevelt was a distant cousin of Teddy Roosevelt.

George Washington was a half first cousin twice removed of James Madison, a second cousin seven times removed of Queen Elizabeth II, a third cousin twice removed of Robert E. Lee, and an eighth cousin six times removed of Winston Churchill.

In 1772, Thomas Jefferson married Martha Wyles Skelton and later inherited her father's land and 135 slaves, including the Hemmings family. In 1782, Thomas Jefferson's wife died and he never remarried. Martha (nicknamed Patsy) and Maria (Mary or nicknamed Polly), two of Jefferson's six children, lived to adulthood.

Through his mother's father, Thomas Jefferson could claim descent from King Edward I of England.

John Tyler, 10th U.S. president, fathered fifteen children—more than any other president. Eight were by his first wife, and seven by his second wife. Tyler was past his 70th birthday when his fifteenth child was born. His son John Tyler, born during Washington's presidency, had several children, the youngest of which lived to see Harry S. Truman become president.

George W. Bush's mother, Barbara Pierce Bush, is the fourth cousin four times removed of Franklin Pierce. Her son is therefore a fourth cousin five times removed of Pierce. Their common ancestor lived from 1618 to 1683.

Most people think that because Lincoln began his life in a log cabin, he was born in poverty. In fact, many families lived in log cabins during the early 1800s. The Lincolns were as comfortable as their neighbors, with their two children, Abraham and Sarah, being well fed and well clothed for the era.

Martin Van Buren was the first president not born a British subject or even of British descent. Like the Roosevelts, the Van Burens were of Dutch descent. His father, Abraham Van Buren, ran a tavern where politicians traveling between New York and Albany often gathered.

These presidents were related to each other: John Adams was the father of John Quincy Adams. James Madison and Zachary Taylor were second cousins. William Henry Harrison was the grandfather of Benjamin Harrison. Franklin D. Roosevelt was a fifth cousin of Theodore Roosevelt. George W. Bush is the son of George H. W. Bush.

Mary Todd Lincoln believed it her duty, as First Lady, to set an example by being the best-dressed woman in the nation. Like the queens of Europe, she purchased far more dresses and dress-making material than she could ever use. Her extravagance put her husband in debt.

The ancestry of all forty-three presidents is limited to one or more of these seven European origins—English, Irish, Scottish, Welsh, Swiss, Dutch, or German.

Woody Guthrie, a famous folk singer, was named after Woodrow Wilson. His full name is Woodrow Wilson Guthrie.

Famous U.S. boxer Jack Dempsey was named after President William Henry Harrison. His real name was William Harrison Dempsey.

Harry S. Truman's middle name is simply "S." As he explained it: "I was supposed to be named Harrison Shippe Truman, taking the middle name from my paternal grandfather. Others in my family wanted my middle name to be Solomon, taken from my maternal grandfather. But apparently no agreement could be reached and my name was recorded and stands simply as Harry S. Truman." Some people leave off the period following the S since the middle name is simply "S" and not an initial that stands for a full middle name.

At the commencement address at Baylor University in 1965, President Lyndon B. Johnson remarked, "This is a moment that I deeply wish my parents could have lived to share. My father would have enjoyed what you have so generously said of me— and my mother would have believed it."

Harry S. Truman wrote a famous angry letter to music critic of the *Washington Post* Paul Hume. After the critic panned, in his column, the president's daughter Margaret's singing debut, Truman advised Hume in a letter that if they ever met, Hume would need "a new nose, a lot of beefsteak for black eyes, and perhaps a supporter below."

Teddy Roosevelt loved the outdoors and pets. He collected over fifty pets for his children, including a badger, macaw, owl, flying squirrel, raccoon, coyote, lion, hyena, zebra, five bears, and a variety of snakes.

Franklin D. Roosevelt was related, either by blood or by marriage, to eleven former presidents.

John C. Breckinridge, the vice president under Buchanan, was also a candidate for president in 1860 and a relation of Mary Todd Lincoln. He later became secretary of war for the Confederacy.

John F. Kennedy said, "I'm not going to appoint ambassadors on the basis of campaign contributions."

A few months later, he added, "Ever since I said that, I haven't gotten a single cent from my father."

Abraham Lincoln's father, Thomas Lincoln, worked as a carpenter making cabinets, door frames, and even coffins. Abraham's mother Nancy Hanks Lincoln was a seamstress who sometimes lived with the families she worked for.

English was not President Martin Van Buren's native tongue. He grew up speaking Dutch.

The mothers of Andrew Jackson and Rutherford B. Hayes died during childbirth.

Abraham Lincoln's mother died at the age of 34 from milk sickness, a disease contracted by drinking milk from cows that have grazed on poisonous white snakeroot. In later years, Abraham would recall helping his father carve pegs for his mother's coffin.

Abraham Lincoln's grandfather, also named Abraham Lincoln, was a captain in the American Revolution.

Dwight D. Eisenhower's parents belonged to a fundamentalist Christian sect known as the River Brethren.

Herbert Hoover lost both of his parents by the time he was nine years old.

Jimmy Carter's mother, Lillian Gordy Carter, joined the Peace Corps at age 68.

The *Baby Ruth* candy bar is named after Grover Cleveland's first daughter, Ruth Cleveland.

Thomas Jefferson made a provision in his will for freeing five slaves upon his death. Three slaves were freed immediately upon his death. Two others were to be freed when they reached the age of 16. Historians note that Jefferson's estate was in debt, which made it impossible to free the rest of his slaves.

George Washington made a provision in his will to free one slave on his death and all the others after the death of his wife Martha. In his will he offered freedom and gave an annuity of $30 to a slave named William Lee, "...as testimony of his attachment to me, and for his faithful services...."

Twelve American presidents, eight of them while serving as president, had owned slaves. Zachary Taylor (1849–1850) was the last president to own slaves while in office.

Ulysses S. Grant's brother Orville was indicted in the whiskey fraud scandals (cheating the government out of whiskey tax revenue) during the Grant administration.

Jimmy Carter's brother, Billy Carter, was accused of being an unlicensed foreign agent of Libya. Although he was not convicted of anything, he made the headlines during Carter's run for reelection in 1980.

John Adams was married longer than any other president. His marriage to Abigail Smith Adams lasted 54 years and 3 months.

Honoring the wish of his wife, Martha Skelton Jefferson, Thomas Jefferson never remarried after her death.

William Henry Harrison and his wife, Anna Symmes, were the first and only presidential couple to elope.

Andrew Jackson married Rachel Donelson while she was still legally married to Lewis Robards from a prominent Kentucky family. She had separated from Robards after he agreed to file a petition for divorce. But after two years of marriage to Jackson, she learned that Robards had not obtained the divorce, but only permission to file for one. Robards brought suit on the grounds of adultery, which was dismissed. After the divorce was granted, the Jacksons quietly remarried in 1794.

After her husband's death, the widow of James K. Polk dressed in mourning black for the rest of her life.

John Tyler was the first president to marry while in office. He married his second wife, Julia Gardiner, in 1844 in New York City.

Andrew Johnson had the youngest bride of any president. He married 16-year-old Eliza McCardle in 1827.

Ulysses S. Grant's parents refused to attend his wedding because the family of his betrothed owned slaves. His bride-to-be, Julia Dent, was from Saint Louis, Missouri.

Grover Cleveland was the only president whose wedding ceremony took place in the White House. In 1886, he married Frances Folsom.

George Washington's granddaughter married Robert E. Lee, who was also his third cousin twice removed.

President John Tyler's widow lived in New York during the Civil War but was a Confederate sympathizer.

Abraham Lincoln's brother-in-law was a surgeon in the Confederate army. Mary Todd Lincoln's full brother, Dr. George Rogers Clark Todd, went South in 1861 to serve as surgeon in a Confederate hospital in Camden, South Carolina.

The Bush family is remotely related to the Spencer family, of which Princess Diana of Wales was a member.

Harry S. Truman ordered John Eisenhower home from overseas military service in Korea so that he could attend the inauguration of his father, Dwight D. Eisenhower.

John Adams had no teeth—a secret his wife and children kept until well after his death.

Theodore Roosevelt's side of the family pronounced the "Roo–" in Roosevelt as in the word *roof*. Franklin D. Roosevelt's side of the family pronounced it as in the word *rose*.

In her later years, William Howard Taft's mother wore a cap to conceal baldness.

Through his mother, Taft was a seventh cousin twice removed of Richard Nixon.

President William Howard Taft and his family were the last residents of the White House to keep a milk cow. The cow, known as Wooly-Mooly and named Pauline Wayne, grazed on the White House grounds.

John F. Kennedy's grandfather—John "Honey Fitz" Fitzgerald—was a saloon keeper and the former mayor of Boston.

President George W. Bush likes to keep in touch with family members and friends through e-mail. Recipients say that his messages are brief and cheerful. He signs off as "gwb."

Abraham Lincoln was reportedly interested in parapsychology and séances in his later years. He wanted to contact former presidents and deceased family members.

Sarah Polk served as her husband's private secretary during his administration and was very active in his political life.

Eleanor Roosevelt, the wife of Franklin D. Roosevelt, was fond of séances. She reported a warm "spiritual friendship" with Abraham Lincoln.

Sarah Polk, worried that her husband's presence would go unnoticed upon entering a room, arranged for the Marine Band to announce the president's arrival by playing an old Scottish anthem, "Hail to The Chief." This established a custom that is observed to this day.

So far in U.S. presidential history, Abigail Adams and Barbara Bush are the only women to have been the wife of one president and the mother of another.

Sarah Polk, wife of President James Polk, set a new style of entertainment. She allowed neither dancing nor drinking (not even wine) at dinner parties. She regarded formal receptions as tedious and often retired early, leaving the president to entertain his guests alone.

Harriet Lane, James Buchanan's niece, served as First Lady to the bachelor president. As hostess in the White House, she returned to the custom of formal dinners and receptions. Americans were once again being entertained at parties in the president's house. Harriet set new fashions in dress, babies were named after her, and the song "Listen to the Mockingbird" was dedicated to her.

Lucy Hayes, wife of President Rutherford B. Hayes, was the first presidential wife to have a college degree. She insisted that prayers be recited at breakfast and encouraged the staff to join her in singing hymns each Sunday evening. She was nicknamed "Lemonade Lucy" because she and her husband banned alcohol, profanity, dancing, and card parties at the White House. One prominent guest at a White House dinner said: "It was a brilliant affair; the water flowed like champagne."

Frances Cleveland, wife of President Grover Cleveland, was considered at the time to be the nation's most beautiful and glamorous woman. When walking around Washington, she was often mobbed by crowds.

William McKinley's wife Ida had epilepsy, which was considered untreatable and incurable at the time. At official functions, the president would always sit by his wife. In the event she would have a seizure, he would place a napkin over her face to conceal her contortions.

When William Howard Taft was elected to the presidency, his wife Nellie had many ideas for improving Washington and the White House. She is best remembered for planting the cherry trees along Washington's tidal basin. The trees were donated by the Mayor of Tokyo.

Grace Coolidge, the wife of Calvin Coolidge, had a strong interest in baseball and was a devoted fan of the Boston Red Sox. She became one of the most popular First Ladies in history.

Grace Coolidge invited many former students of the Clarke School and other hearing-impaired people to the White House.

Ellen Wilson, first wife of President Woodrow Wilson, lobbied for improvements for women and African-

Americans living in Washington, D.C. She was responsible for passing slum-clearance legislation called the Ellen Wilson bill.

In 2004, *Forbes* magazine named Laura Bush the fourth most powerful woman in the world.

What's in a Name?

Grover Cleveland's birth name was Stephen Cleveland. He hated the near-rhyme and, while still in his twenties, dropped the name "for something more important sounding."

William "Bill" Clinton was born with the name William Jefferson Blythe IV. Bill never knew his father, who died in an auto accident before his son was born. When Bill was 4 years old, his mother married Roger Clinton. At age 14, Bill formally changed his last name to that of his stepfather.

Calvin Coolidge also thought he needed a better star-quality name. He dropped the use of his first name, John, in his twenties.

Woodrow Wilson also did not like his first name, Thomas, which he dropped in "search for something more important and distinctive."

Dwight D. Eisenhower was born David Dwight Eisenhower, but later reversed his first and middle names.

President Gerald Ford was born Leslie Lynch King, but when his father died, his mother remarried. King took his adoptive father's name, Gerald Ford.

Ulysses S. Grant was born Hiram Ulysses Grant. When he entered the Military Academy he was mistakenly registered as "Ulysses Simpson Grant" and he preferred it to his birth name.

The First Feminist, Abigail Adams

Abigail Adams may have been the first woman in the United States to stand up for women's rights. In one of her many letters to her husband when he was in Congress, she wrote: "Remember the ladies, and be more generous and favorable to them than your ancestors...If particular care is not paid to the ladies, we are determined to foment a rebellion, and will not hold ourselves bound by any laws in which we have no voice, or representation."

Abigail Adams was a great woman of strong convictions, wonderful intellect, masterful writing and outstanding wisdom. Not only was she instrumental in the careers of her husband and son, but she was also an inspiration to women's rights activists.

Lou Henry

Lou Henry, wife of President Herbert Hoover, was the first woman to graduate from Stanford University with a degree in geology. She met Herbert Hoover in the geology lab at Stanford University.

Lou and Herbert Hoover married on February 10, 1899, in Monterey, California. For their honeymoon, they sailed to China because Hoover was en route to join a mining company in China. There Mrs. Hoover learned Chinese.

After Lou Hoover invited Mrs. Oscar DePriest, the wife of an African-American congressman from Chicago, for tea, she was criticized by the press. The incident caused a great commotion in Washington and the nation. She was praised by some and condemned by others.

Eleanor Roosevelt

Eleanor Roosevelt, wife of Franklin D. Roosevelt, loved flying. Before becoming First Lady, she flew for many hundreds of hours. She continued this practice during her husband's presidency, flying to many locations, and acting as an invaluable adviser to him. Eleanor traveled so much that she became known as the "flying First Lady" (as a passenger) and served as a poster child for the airlines industry.

Eleanor Roosevelt once accepted an invitation from the most famous woman pilot of the time, Amelia Earhart, to fly with her over the Capitol at night. For the event, Amelia even wore a long evening dress at the controls.

Eleanor Roosevelt was known to purchase ten-dollar dresses rather than indulge in more extravagant dress. When a *New York Times* reporter speculated that she spent less than $300 one year on her wardrobe, she proudly saved the newspaper article in her scrapbook.

Eleanor Roosevelt held a White House press conference for women reporters. This was unheard of at the time because prior to Eleanor, women reporters were barred from attending White House press events.

Irish Roots

The first president of Irish descent was Andrew Jackson, whose parents, Andrew Jackson and Elizabeth Hutchinson, were born in Carrickfergus, County Antrim, in Northern Ireland.

James K. Polk was also of Irish descent. His great-great grandfather, Robert Pollock, from County Donegal, emigrated to Maryland and changed his name to Polk.

James Buchanan was of Irish descent. His father was born in County Donegal, also the ancestral home of James K. Polk.

Ulysses S. Grant's mother was the granddaughter of John Simpson, who was born in Northern Ireland about 1738.

The great-great-great grandfather of William McKinley was born in Ireland in 1705 and emigrated to America.

The grandfather of Woodrow Wilson was born in Strabane, County Down, Ireland, in 1787.

John F. Kennedy relished his Irish heritage. His father's great-grandparents were Patrick Kennedy, born in Dunganstown, County Wexford, about 1823, and Bridget Murphy, born in Owenduff, County Wexford, about 1827. His mother's great grandparents were Thomas Fitzgerald, born in Bruff, County Limerick, in 1823, and Rose Anna Cox, born in County Cavan, in 1835.

Even though they campaigned against each other for the presidency, John F. Kennedy and Richard Nixon had a secret liking for each other, possibly because they shared an Irish heritage. Nixon was descended from James Moore, born in Ballymoney, County Antrim, in 1777. Another ancestor, Thomas Milhous, was born in Carrickfergus, County Antrim (ancestral home of Andrew Jackson), in 1699.

Ronald Reagan also delighted in his Irish roots. His great grandfather, Michael Reagan, was from County Tipperary, emigrated to Canada, and then moved to the United States. Michael's wife, Catherine Mulcahey, was also born in Ireland.

Chapter 6
Presidential Food and Drink

You probably know that George H. W. Bush hates broccoli, but did you also know that Franklin Roosevelt loved moose meat and grape jelly? The dining habits of American presidents have fascinated the American public for years. Imagine Herbert Hoover sitting down to his favorite supper—corned beef hash with tomato sauce—lovingly prepared by his wife Lou. And does a watermelon-seed spitting contest sound like appropriate behavior at the president's dining table? President Truman and his daughter Margaret thought so.

President Teddy Roosevelt was a big eater and had a sweet tooth. He put as many as six sugar cubes in a single cup of coffee. However, Teddy's cup was quite large; a breakfast guest once observed that it looked like a bathtub.

President Eisenhower was said to be a talented cook, often preparing meals for his guests. His wife, Mamie, was noted as being thrifty and made sure all the leftovers were used. She was proud of saying she could squeeze a dollar so tight you could hear the eagle (on the U.S. silver dollar) scream.

Almost all U.S. presidents did drink some alcohol. To date, three presidents have admitted to having problems with alcohol. They are Franklin Pierce, Ulysses S. Grant, and George W. Bush.

Franklin Pierce was arrested for running over an elderly woman while driving his horse-drawn carriage when drunk. The charges were dropped in 1853 for insufficient evidence.

"I do not like broccoli. And I haven't liked it since I was a little kid and my mother made me eat it. And I'm president of the United States, and I'm not going to eat any more broccoli."—George H. W. Bush

The Reagan Administration considered ketchup as a vegetable when determining minimum nutritional guidelines for school lunches.

According to a collection of menus in the archives of the White House, Benjamin Harrison's wife, Caroline, prepared the family turkey in a unique way. She fed the bird a walnut and gave it a shot of sherry at least three times a day.

Ulysses S. Grant hired an Army cook as the White House chef. The cook's recipe collection was limited to fowl, usually turkey, and state dinners had become an embarrassment. Mrs. Grant finally persuaded her husband to hire a chef from Italy.

Was George Washington poisoned? A story about Washington widely told but never confirmed: Washington's faithful cook considered him disloyal for rebelling against the King of England. The cook hoped to kill Washington by adding tomatoes—then considered poisonous—to Washington's favorite stew. While George was enjoying the stew, the cook went outside and shot himself. Many years later, a suicide note was found behind the fireplace.

Eleanor and Franklin D. Roosevelt were among the most socially active of all the First Families. The Roosevelt White House provided dinner parties and entertainment for over 10,000 people in 1937 alone.

President Thomas Jefferson, a great connoisseur of food and wine, collected many recipes from abroad. Whenever he liked a dish, he would ask the chef for the recipe. There was no refusing Jefferson. He was said to be relentless until he got the chef to give it up.

The night of Grant's second inaugural ball was so bitterly cold that many guests danced wearing their coats. Much of the food prepared for guests froze solid.

Franklin D. Roosevelt had a favorite exotic dish— moose meat with grape jelly.

The inaugural ball for William Henry
Harrison featured an 800-pound
cake in the shape of the U.S. Capitol.

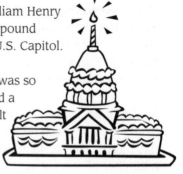

President Calvin Coolidge was so
fond of chicken that he had a
chicken coop and yard built
behind the White House.
Food writers of the time
reported that those who'd
tasted Coolidge's chickens raved about their wonderful
and mysterious flavor. After much speculation, it was
later discovered that the chicken coops and yard were
built over Teddy Roosevelt's mint patch.

President George W. Bush was in Scotland for his
birthday. He was asked if he wanted haggis, the
national dish of Scotland. "I was briefed on haggis,"
he said. "Generally on your birthday, you—my mother
used to say, 'What do you want to eat?' And I don't
ever remember saying, 'Haggis, Mom.'"

President and Mrs. Harding loved to entertain. Soon
after the inauguration, Mrs. Harding had the White

House silverware sent off to be triple gold-plated. The entertainment bills were so high that the Hardings had to economize on all other expenses. President Harding thought he could help by turning off every other lightbulb in the White House.

In May 1966, Lyndon B. Johnson received a note from his cook which he shared with his wife and daughters: "Mr. President, you have been my boss for a number of years. And you always tell me you want to lose weight, and yet you never do very much to help yourself. Now I'm going to be your boss for a change. Eat what I put in front of you, don't ask for any more, and don't complain."

President Harry S. Truman and his wife sometimes held watermelon-seed spitting contests with their daughter, Margaret. (Presumably this took place at picnic tables outdoors and the seeds landed in spots where

they could take root.) They also playfully threw bits of bread at each other at the White House table.

At George and Martha Washington's Mount Vernon estate, dinner was served at 3 o'clock in the afternoon. The plainest meal would consist of three courses. For fancier dinners, as many as twenty different dishes would be served. The prevailing custom—among the aristocrats whose customs they emulated—was that a good hostess would provide enough dishes to completely hide the tablecloth.

According to his own writings, Tuesday was not George Washington's favorite day. The Tuesday dinner and reception was a very stuffy affair, requiring the president to shake the hands of many guests. But he didn't like to shake hands. He avoided the problem by standing in the reception line, holding his hat in one hand, while he placed his other hand on his sword. He simply gave his guests a slight bow.

George Washington's mother, Mary Washington, was famous for her gingerbread, which she claimed was based on a recipe dating from the Roman Empire.

Washington's Veal and Bacon Pie

This recipe was found in the Mount Vernon library. You can find all of the ingredients in a supermarket.

Ingredients

- 11 to 12 ounces of pastry dough
- ¼ pound bacon, 1½ pounds veal, cubed
- salt and pepper
- yolks of 4 hard-boiled eggs
- ½ tablespoon parsley
- ½ teaspoon thyme
- ½ teaspoon marjoram
- 1 uncooked egg white
- 2 tablespoons butter
- ½ teaspoon savory

Directions: Line one 9-inch pie pan with half of the pastry dough. Cook bacon and crumble over meat. Season with salt and pepper and place into pastry. Mix egg yolks and spices. Bind with egg white and mix with meat. Dot with butter. Place remaining pastry over the top. Bake for about one hour or until crust is brown. Serves 8–10.

Note: Savory is a Mediterranean herb with pale lavender and white aromatic leaves, probably grown in the Mount Vernon greenhouse.

She often baked it for dinners, including one thrown in honor of French General Lafayette. The recipe was passed down to many other First Families. The Lincoln papers indicate that Abe himself loved Mary's gingerbread recipe and had the White House chef prepare it regularly.

In Washington's day, butter was churned by hand. Most people raised their own farm animals to obtain meat, milk, or eggs. Many people also had a vegetable garden and grew herbs for cooking and medicinal purposes. Spices were rare and considered luxury items.

Thomas Jefferson is credited for introducing various spices to the American palette. Cinnamon, clove, black pepper, and anise were all novel flavors brought back from France and presented at state dinners to amazed guests.

Thomas Jefferson was mostly a vegetarian. He ate very little meat. His diet included a lot of vegetables, fruits, and nuts. He was known for collecting seeds and cultivating many different plants for the White House table.

After one of the many fancy dinners at Mount Vernon, George Washington was warming himself, standing with his back to the fire. The fire got too hot and Washington moved away. A guest noticed this and said, "A general should be able to stand the heat." Noting Washington's displeasure at the comment, the guest quickly added, "But a wise general should not take too much fire from behind."

How long does it take to prepare a state dinner? The White House chef and staff begin planning a state dinner two months in advance. They prepare a tasting dinner for the First Lady and note her comments. Then they submit a revised menu and schedule a second tasting. They order food about one and a half weeks before the dinner and begin preparation two days in advance. Most of the actual cooking takes place within two hours of service time.

Spoon bread, a type of corn porridge, is one of the earliest types of food that Native Americans introduced to the settlers at Jamestown, Virginia. Its high carbohydrate value provided excellent sustenance for the settlers in times when meat and other vegetables were scarce. Andrew Jackson improved the recipe with the addition of molasses and served it regularly at White House dinners. His delighted guests called it Indian Sweet Pudding.

When James Monroe became president, the White House was still under repair from fires set by the British during the War of 1812. Mrs. Monroe had to redecorate and replace everything, including the kitchen. As a woman with impeccable taste, she chose kitchenware from France. She even purchased gold-plated silverware that had once belonged to Marie Antoinette.

After refurbishing the White House kitchen, Mrs. James Monroe hired a French chef and insisted on French cuisine for all meals. In keeping with this, dinner hour was changed from 4:00 P.M. to the more fashionable French hour of 6:00 P.M. White House guests grew tired of the unrelenting French cuisine, and complaints began to leak to the press. An article in a local paper, noted in the Monroe papers, declared, "French cooking prevailed much to the disgust of many prominent officials." Monroe's own staff complained about the food and that the atmosphere at White House dinners was too formal and strict.

For state dinners, Mrs. James Monroe decorated tables with wax flowers. In those days, people thought fresh flowers were carriers of disease.

After one formal dinner in the Van Buren White House, guests were relaxing and enjoying cheese wafers. A panicky servant rushed in to tell President Van Buren that the kitchen was on fire. Van Buren went to the kitchen, helped put out the fire, and then returned to his guests, one of whom was Henry Clay, his political opponent. Clay stood up, placed his hand over his heart, and declared "Mr. President, while I admit I am doing all I can to remove you from this house, please believe me. I am not trying to burn you out."

In the first half of the 19th century, political campaigns often used food and drink to bribe voters. In 1840, William Henry Harrison held an enormous public picnic that included 360 hams, 1,500 pounds of beef, scores of sheep and calves, 4,500 pies and many barrels of hard cider. The Harrison slogan was: "Log Cabin and Hard Cider."

William Henry Harrison was the only president who actually did the grocery shopping for the White House. He wanted to be sure he got the best cuts of meat. He was known to go to the market alone wearing old clothes and a big floppy hat.

In 1845, President James Polk and his family hosted the first formal Thanksgiving dinner at the White House. Since then, all presidents host an official White House Thanksgiving dinner.

If your Thanksgiving dinner includes popovers, a thin-crusted egg biscuit, you are having what the

White House is serving. Popovers have been part of the traditional White House menu since the time of James Polk.

Before becoming president, Zachary Taylor was a soldier serving in Louisiana, where he learned to love Cajun food. While president, he introduced Cajun dishes at state dinners. Guests thought the fare "homely, but novel" and consumed it with delight. Today, Taylor is credited for adding Cajun cuisine to the American palette.

President Zachary Taylor was said to be very picky about hominy made from the best sweet corn. When Taylor found out that his horse could sniff out bags of the best hominy corn, he would take his horse to the Army grain storehouse. When the horse chewed a hole in a particular bag, that bag was hauled off to the White House kitchen.

Before the time of President Millard Fillmore, food at the White House was cooked over open fires. Fillmore and his wife Abigail had the first cast-iron stove installed. The White House staff had no idea how to use this "fad gimmick." Fillmore himself had to go to the patent office to find out how the stove worked.

Franklin Pierce was known to be a party animal. He was good-looking, hard-drinking, and very successful. When his wife was ill, he hosted state dinners by himself. One of the most popular dishes served in the Pierce White House was his clam soup. Pierce had the recipe published in a local newspaper for all to see—in verse!

President James Buchanan, a picky eater, only ate butter churned in Philadelphia and sent to the White House weekly in a locked kettle. His niece Harriet Lane, who served as First Lady, began a relationship with a man in Philadelphia. Because Buchanan did not approve of him, Harriet secretly communicated by exchanging notes placed in the butter kettle. Harriet retrieved the letters before the president knew about them. The two would-be lovers reportedly carried on the relationship for a long time. The butter-kettle notes were never discovered.

When Andrew Johnson was president, life in the White House was not exactly all glamour. His daughter Martha had to churn all the butter for the family and staff.

President Hayes adored animal paintings. He ordered that the official dinnerware be decorated with animals—deer, buffalo, opossums, raccoons, and squirrels. Antique dealers highly prize the surviving chinaware.

James Garfield hosted one of the largest inauguration parties in our history. Because there were far too many guests to fit into one building at the same time, 500 guests had to be served at a time in several seatings.

Chester A. Arthur makes the list of White House party animals. Arthur sometimes quit work at 11:00 P.M. and impulsively decided to throw a party for his Washington buddies. The chef was awakened and word went out: "Come on over!"
Whenever Chester A. Arthur traveled by rail, he

brought his personal chef, favorite wines, fanciest china, and silverware.

When Grover Cleveland succeeded Chester A. Arthur, Cleveland was disgusted with the overly fancy cuisine of his predecessor. Cleveland was heard to say, "I would rather eat pickled herring, Swiss cheese, and a chop at Louis's instead of all this French fare." Arthur's cook was soon replaced with one who suited the new president's tastes.

President Benjamin Harrison was crazy for oysters and even had them for breakfast. Oysters were very popular in Harrison's time and were sold in the streets like hot dogs at a ballgame. He came up with an improved method for smoking oysters that's still used today.

Bubble and Squeak, another name for corned beef and cabbage, was Grover Cleveland's favorite dish. Some speculate that the curious name comes from the sound cabbage makes while cooking. Others attribute the name to digestive murmurings.

Guests dining at the Grover Cleveland White House received a souvenir. Women were given a ribbon with their name, date, and a picture of the White House seal. Men were given a similar but smaller version of the ribbon.

William McKinley loved Lobster Newburg, a rich fare made with diced lobster, heavy cream, butter, and very expensive truffles, still served in fancy restaurants today. The McKinley family also had a special recipe for cole slaw that included cream, butter, and eggs.

While Teddy Roosevelt was a big chocolate lover, his other favorite flavor was mint, and he always kept mint chocolates in his office. He loved mint jelly and mint juleps. In order to indulge his appetite for mint, he had mint planted in the White House gardens.

One of Teddy Roosevelt's favorite desserts was Picket Fence Pudding, made from chocolate, cream, egg yolks, and lady fingers. The lady fingers were placed, fencelike, around the rich pudding. The White House chef reputedly created this dessert for Teddy, combining his favorite treats into a new dessert.

Teddy Roosevelt's daughter Alice's wedding cake weighed over 130 pounds.

Like her husband Teddy, Edith Roosevelt also loved sweets. Her specialty was Sagamore Hill Sand Tarts, butter-rich sugar cookies. For holidays, Mrs. Roosevelt herself prepared hundreds of cookies for the family and guests.

One of Taft's favorite dishes was Runnymede Salad, named for the English field on which King John of England signed the Magna Carta. This meal-in-itself salad contained shrimp, potatoes, eggs, mushrooms, artichoke hearts, cucumbers, and lots of mayonnaise.

In 1917, President Woodrow Wilson's chef created War Bread to demonstrate a no-frills menu at the White House in support of the war effort. The bread contained rye and whole-wheat flour, raisins, and molasses. Breakfast guests at the White House presumably found it delicious.

President Wilson kept sheep on the White House grounds reportedly to save the cost of mowing the lawns. From the sheep, wool was supposedly given to the Army to make blankets for soldiers. The animals also provided mutton for the White House tables; beef was reserved for the military.

During the Harding Administration, the Eighteenth Amendment (Prohibition) was in force, banning the sale and consumption of alcohol. This did not prevent Mrs. Harding from serving her famous Bourbon Balls, made with smuggled liquor, to White House guests.

Calvin Coolidge's nickname was Silent Cal because he spoke so little. Even so, gatherings at the Coolidge White House had lots of lively after-dinner conversation. A dinner guest, the legend goes, made a bet that she could get the president to say at least three words. Coolidge's reply was, "You lose."

Corned-beef hash with tomato sauce was Herbert Hoover's favorite dish. Mrs. Hoover served it to him whenever the president appeared tense and upset.

To improve her memory, Eleanor Roosevelt supposedly took the advice of her doctor, who suggested she eat three chocolate-covered garlic cloves every day!

Eleanor Roosevelt enjoyed cooking scrambled eggs. At White House breakfasts, the staff prepared a special chafing dish so that she could take the order of each guest and scramble eggs to their liking.

Eleanor Roosevelt once held a picnic at Hyde Park in London for Queen Elizabeth II and her husband. Eleanor planned to serve hot dogs, but this infuriated her mother-in-law. Eleanor refused to be bullied into serving more regal fare and stuck to her original menu. The Hormel Company, which provided the hot dogs, was so impressed by Eleanor's perseverance that they invited her to appear in a print ad.

Harry S. Truman hated fancy food. He called himself a meat-and-potatoes man. He disliked anything with cucumbers and onions.

Bess Truman, wife of President Harry S. Truman, was an excellent pastry chef and famous for her brownies.

President Dwight D. Eisenhower was a big fan of beef stew and vegetable soup. He prepared them at White House dinners for close friends.

Mamie Eisenhower made magnificent fudge for her husband and friends. Ike called it million-dollar fudge. Legend has it that the fudge was shipped aboard airplanes bound for secret war missions.

President Lyndon B. Johnson was a chili connoisseur. Many functions at the LBJ Ranch included a kettle of his famous Perdernales River Chili. The recipe was a secret, and the president himself often sneaked into the kitchen to guard against food spies and ensure that his cook prepared the chili to perfection.

Occasionally, a new chef erred, and Johnson could be heard yelling, "No beans, please! Beans have no place in a proper Texas chili!" The president's aides advised all those seeking favors to understand Johnson's "barbecue diplomacy" and partake in his chili meals with delight and enthusiasm.

Fish chowder was a big Kennedy family favorite. John F. Kennedy liked his chowder so much that he took a large thermos^{TM} of chowder with him when he traveled.

Jackie Kennedy gave elegant parties. For one state dinner, guests were taken on a yacht up the Potomac River to Mount Vernon, to dine. Dinner ended with Jackie's favorite dessert,
crème brûlée, served on the terrace.

A Lyndon and Lady Bird Johnson White House dinner would often include some country dancing. LBJ was said to be one of our best dancing presidents. Jackie Kennedy once said he was her favorite partner.

Although he described himself as a simple man raised on Quaker values and plain food, Richard Nixon's White House had over 50,000 guests in the first year. The meals were lavish and a favorite dish was Beef Wellington.

Shortly after moving into the White House, Richard Nixon and his daughter Tricia requested a snack from the White House kitchen. The president requested tomato juice and cottage cheese while his daughter demanded a simple hot dog with mustard. The kitchen staff, bewildered and embarrassed by the requests, had to run to a local delicatessen to purchase the items. Ever since that time, the White House kitchen has had an ample supply of cottage cheese, tomato juice, and hot dogs.

One of the stranger dishes the Nixons enjoyed was Pat Nixon's chicken salad with potato chips. The chips were crumbled into the chicken and mayonnaise mixture for a gooey-crunchy treat.

Gerald Ford was perhaps the least fussy president when it came to food. He ate anything and lots of it. He once said: "I will eat anything slow enough for me to catch. And, if I can get it on an English muffin, that would be heaven."

Peanut Pie—a mixture of peanut butter cookies, peanuts, molasses, and eggs—was the favorite dessert in the Carter White House. Peanuts played such a role in Carter's life that *Air Force One* was nicknamed "Peanut One."

During the Carter White House, the chef took a crash course in how to prepare a favorite snack: cheddar-cheese grits. The grits recipe became a fad in Virginia; many restaurants offered it on their menus.

White House guests were sometimes surprised to be invited by President Clinton to join him on a midnight refrigerator raid. Sometimes butlers and other staff members joined Clinton to have a sandwich and watch late-night sports on the kitchen television.

When the Clintons moved into the White House, it lacked a real eat-in family kitchen. Hillary Clinton had one installed next to the official dining room. The Clinton family preferred family-style meals around a small table and American-style cooking. To underscore his love of American cuisine at a dinner following a NATO conference, President Clinton made sure American bison (buffalo) was on the menu.

According to former First Lady Hillary Clinton, preparations for the White House Christmas dinner would begin as early as April.

As First Lady, Hillary Clinton once joked that she could have stayed home, baking cookies and hosting teas, but preferred an active career. She took lots of heat from women who interpreted this comment as critical of women who chose to stay at home to raise their families. Hillary apologized, and to underscore the apology, baked cookies and had them served to reporters at a press conference. Later, thousands of Hillary's cookies were handed out at the 1992 Democratic National Convention. Her chocolate chip cookie recipe got top honors from *Family Circle* magazine, beating out those baked by Republican competitors Barbara Bush and Elizabeth Dole.

George W. Bush was proud of his abilities in the kitchen. He often made pancakes and omelets with his two daughters.

For one very important diplomatic event, the Russian President Vladimir Putin and his wife were invited to George and Laura Bush's Texas ranch. The menu included mesquite-smoked beef tenderloin, southern-fried catfish, and a special Blue Bell vanilla ice cream. Laura Bush is famous for her extra-rich hot chocolate. On very cold nights, guests have been known to put off leaving until they're offered a taste of Mrs. Bush's treat.

Chapter 7

Presidents and Their Houses

For many American presidents, the White House was a step down. James Madison galloped across the 8,000 acres of his estate in Virginia, Montpelier, long before he and Dolley moved into the mansion on the Potomac River. John F. Kennedy tossed footballs across the lawns of mansions up and down the East Coast before settling into the Executive Mansion. And then there was Jefferson's Monticello—probably the grandest retirement home ever built. Still, the address 1600 Pennsylvania Avenue held a certain appeal.

The White House

A Few Statistics on the White House

The White House has 132 rooms, including 35 baths, 412 doors, 28 fireplaces, eight staircases, and three elevators. Six floors comprise "the residence" of the White House, which does not include areas of the building reserved for administration of the executive branch. The entire complex occupies 18 acres of land.

For recreation, the White House has a variety of facilities available to its residents, including a tennis court, jogging track, swimming pool, movie theater, and bowling lane.

With five full-time chefs, the White House kitchen is able to serve dinner to as many as 140 guests and hors d'oeuvres to more than 1,000.

The White House requires 570 gallons of paint to cover its outside surface.

The White House Under Construction

In December 1790, President George Washington signed an Act of Congress declaring that the federal government would be relocated to what is today

Washington, D.C. President Washington, together with the very talented French city planner, Pierre L'Enfant, chose the site for the new national capital with a district "not exceeding ten miles square...on the river Potomac." The street address we know today is 1600 Pennsylvania Avenue, and the district is Washington, D.C.

Nine architects competed for the design of the original White House. The winner was Irish-born architect James Hoban, who was awarded a gold medal for his "practical and handsome design."

Construction on the original White House began when the first cornerstone was laid in October of 1792. Washington oversaw construction of the house but never lived in it.

In 1800, when the mansion was nearly completed, its first residents, President John Adams and his wife, Abigail, moved in.

Living at the White House

When John and Abigail Adams moved into the White House, the lawn lacked a fence, so Abigail hung the family's laundry out to dry in the East Room.

At various times in history, the White House has been known as the "President's Palace," the "President's House," and the "Executive Mansion." In 1812 it was reportedly nicknamed the White House, and in 1901 President Theodore Roosevelt's use made the name official.

In 1798, the building was first made white with lime-based whitewash to protect the porous stone from freezing.

In 1889 when Caroline Harrison, wife of President Benjamin Harrison, moved to Washington, she thought that the White House was in such terrible condition that she tried to talk her husband into tearing it down and replacing it with a more modern residence. She made major improvements to the White House. She was responsible for installing electric lights, new heating, and several bathrooms. Up to that time, the White House had only one private bathroom.

The White House suffered two major fires. In 1814 the British deliberately tried to burn the mansion, and in 1929 during Herbert Hoover's presidency, a fire began by accident in the West Wing.

In the War of 1812, British General Robert Ross burned the White House and Capitol in 1814 in retaliation for the burning of the Canadian Capitol, York (now Toronto). Luckily, an evening rainstorm saved the building from total destruction, and James Hoban, the original architect, renovated the almost gutted building.

When Thomas Jefferson became president in 1801, he turned the State Dining Room into his private office. He admitted very few people into this private space and used the Red Room to meet guests. The only other living creature granted full access to his office was his pet mockingbird.

In the White House, Thomas Jefferson proudly displayed samples of Native American artifacts and American flora and fauna that Meriwether Lewis sent him from the Lewis and Clark expedition. He also displayed similar pieces in Monticello, his Virginia home.

When Andrew Jackson moved into the White House, the State Dining Room was located near the stables. With the windows open, guests had difficulty appreciating the wonderful aromas of the meals served. Jackson ordered that the stables be relocated.

Thomas Jefferson began the tradition of opening the White House for public tours. Except for wartime, the executive mansion has remained open to the public ever since. Jefferson also held open receptions at the White House on New Year's Day and the Fourth of July. He greeted strangers, bowed to ladies, and even kissed babies. The tradition of open receptions on New Year's Day and the Fourth of July continued until the early 1930s.

During the Carter Administration the White House's exterior was renovated. This entailed stripping through 27 layers of paint.

Three massive carved eagles support the concert grand piano by Steinway and Sons installed in the

White House in 1903. The piano was retired to the Smithsonian Museum in 1938.

Like Jefferson, Teddy Roosevelt was a passionate amateur naturalist. During his administration, a moose head graced the State Dining Room.

Franklin D. Roosevelt had a pool built in the White House to use as therapy for his legs that were afflicted with polio. Forty years later, President Nixon had the new Press Briefing Room constructed atop the Roosevelt pool. In 2000 it was renamed the James Brady Press Briefing Room to honor the former White House press secretary, who had been shot and seriously injured during an assassination attempt on President Ronald Reagan in 1981.

The White House gardener caught Quentin Roosevelt, Teddy Roosevelt's son, playing in the ornate flowerbeds. When President Roosevelt scolded Quentin, the child replied, "I don't see what good it does me for you to be president."

One night in 1948, President Harry S. Truman was having a long hot soak, when he noticed the bathtub was dropping through the floor. This precipitated a massive structural renovation that required virtually gutting the entire residential section of the White House.

President Kennedy liked roses so much that he had another rose garden created just outside the Oval Office, designed as a place for outdoor ceremonies.

In 1913, Ellen Wilson, the first wife of Woodrow Wilson, replaced Mrs. Teddy Roosevelt's colonial garden with a rose garden. The West Garden has been known as the Rose Garden ever since.

Throughout much of Harry S. Truman's presidency, the interior of the White House, with the exception of the third floor, was completely gutted and renovated. During the renovation, the Trumans lived across the street at Blair House. Despite the scope of renovation, the contractors were instructed to protect and not alter in any way the stone façade of the mansion, first put into place over two centuries ago.

Jacqueline Kennedy was influential in restoring the interior of the White House with historically appropriate furniture, paintings, and fabrics. She charmed private collectors into donating period pieces for White House rooms. After the early 1960s' renovation, she guided Americans on a televised tour of the White House. Millions watched the hour-long program, and thousands flocked to the White House to look in person.

Jacqueline Kennedy wrote the first White House guidebook, sold to visiting tourists, which raised several million dollars for the White House Historical Association. Under her influence, new laws began to protect the furnishings and forbid presidents from claiming or giving away historic items.

Theodore Roosevelt ordered the construction of a temporary office building to the west of the White House, now known as the West Wing. This change provided more living space inside the White House and made it possible to expand the size of the State Dining Room.

Inaugurations

After his 1805 inauguration, Thomas Jefferson held an open house at the White House. Many people who attended the swearing-in ceremony at the U.S. Capitol simply followed him home, where the new president greeted his guests in the Blue Room.

In 1829 a horde of 20,000 inaugural well-wishers forced President Andrew Jackson to flee the White House for the safety of a hotel. On the White House lawn, aides filled washtubs with orange juice and whiskey to lure the mob out of the mansion and send them home.

After Abraham Lincoln's presidency, the tradition of opening the White House to inaugural crowds continued, even though the crowds had grown too large and difficult to manage.

Grover Cleveland effected better crowd control. He was the first president to substitute a presidential review of the troops from a flag-draped grandstand built in front of the White House. This evolved into the official Inaugural Parade we know today.

Samuel Morse transmitted the inauguration of President James Polk by telegraph in 1845.

The first photographed inauguration was James Buchanan's in 1857, and the first recorded on film and gramophone was William McKinley's in 1897.

In the 20th century, technological firsts were Calvin Coolidge's inauguration broadcast by radio in 1925, Herbert Hoover's on sound newsreel in 1929, and Harry S. Truman's broadcast on television in 1949.

Lincoln's Ghost

Harry S. Truman was once asked if he thought the White House was haunted. His reply: "Sure as shootin' it is."

Many people speculate that Abraham Lincoln's spirit lingers in the White House because of the trauma he endured while in office. Others feel Lincoln appears in times of crisis.

President Lincoln reportedly once told a friend that he dreamed of seeing his own casket in the East Room of the White House. In the dream, Lincoln heard people crying, then wandered into the East Room, where he saw his casket and a room full of mourners. Lincoln asked a guard, "Who died?" and the guard responded, "The president. He was killed by an assassin."

President Harry S. Truman was working after midnight in the Oval Office when a loud knock on the door startled him. He opened the door to find no one there. The knock continued over the past hour and was so disturbing the president stopped his work. The next day Truman described the incident to a friend and speculated that it was "Lincoln's ghost."

Legend has it that Lincoln's ghost returns to the White House when the security of the country is at risk. He strides up and down the second-floor hall-way, knocks at doors, and stands by certain windows with his hands clasped behind his back. One staff member claimed to have seen Lincoln sitting on his bed pulling on his boots.

When a reporter asked Roslyn Carter if she's

ever seen or heard Lincoln's ghost, she refused to comment. But, when Jacqueline Kennedy was asked, she stated that she felt Lincoln's presence many times in or about the Oval Office, and "took great comfort in it."

Grace Coolidge, wife of Calvin Coolidge, was the first person to report having seen Lincoln's ghost in the White House. She said that he stood at a window of the Oval Office, hands clasped behind his back, gazing out over the Potomac.

A bodyguard to President Harrison was kept awake many nights trying to protect the president from mysterious footsteps heard in the hall outside the president's bedroom. The guard grew so tired and worried that he finally attended a séance to beg President Lincoln to stop so he could get enough sleep to properly protect the president.

When a guest of the White House, Queen Wilhelmina of the Netherlands reported hearing a knock on her bedroom door. Upon answering it, she saw Lincoln before her, wearing his famous top hat.

Mary Eben, Eleanor Roosevelt's secretary, also reported seeing Lincoln, sitting on the bed in the

Lincoln bedroom pulling on his boots. Many other staff members during this period also reported seeing him lying on the bed at different times.

Other Ghosts

During the Taft Administration, several White House staff reported seeing a ghostly female figure drifting through the East Room to hang laundry in the hallway outside. The ghost was supposedly Abigail Adams.

Some people have believed that Andrew Jackson still inhabits the White House's Rose Room, where his bed remains to this day. Mary Todd Lincoln reported hearing him stomping around the White House corridors and cursing.

While working, several White House gardeners have been startled by what they described as a young woman in a colorful dress with a large bonnet who scolded them for turning up the soil. Supposedly, the ghost of Dolley Madison was upset about the destruction of the rose bushes she planted over 100 years ago.

The Oval Office

The preference for oval rooms dates back to the time of George Washington. At his home in Philadelphia, Washington had two oval-shaped rooms where he hosted receptions. As guests formed a circle around him, Washington stood in the center to greet them.

President William Howard Taft was the first to create an oval office in the center of the West Wing of the White House. In doing so, Taft felt he was more centrally located and therefore more involved with his administration's day-to-day operations. In 1934, the Oval Office was moved to its current location on the southeast corner, overlooking the Rose Garden.

Each presidential family has decorated the Oval Office to suit its own tastes. Among the features that remain constant are the white marble mantel from the original 1909 Oval Office, the presidential seal in the ceiling, and two flags behind the president's desk (the U.S. flag and the president's flag).

President Woodrow Wilson made the first transcontinental phone call from the Oval Office on January 25, 1915.

The Resolute Desk

In the Oval Office, George W. Bush uses a desk called the Resolute. It was made from the wood of an abandoned British ship, the *H.M.S. Resolute*, which an American ship discovered and returned to England as a token of friendship and goodwill. Queen Victoria commissioned the desk and presented it to President Rutherford B. Hayes in 1880.

The desk was modified twice from the original version. In 1945, President Franklin D. Roosevelt requested that the kneehole be fitted with a panel carved with the presidential coat-of-arms, but he did not live to see it installed.

In 1984, Ronald Reagan requested that the desk be raised on a 2-inch base to accommodate his 6'2" frame. With the exception of Presidents Johnson, Nixon, and Ford, every president since Rutherford B. Hayes has used the Resolute desk. A photograph of President John F. Kennedy at work at the desk, while his son, John, Jr., peeked out from behind the kneehole panel, made the desk world famous.

Camp David

Camp David is a rustic retreat for the president, providing the First Family and their guests with a healthful, safe, and private place to work or relax. Formerly named Shangri-La by President Franklin D. Roosevelt, it was renamed Camp David by Dwight D. Eisenhower after his grandson, David Eisenhower.

Most presidents have used Camp David to host visiting foreign leaders, with Prime Minister Winston Churchill of Great Britain being the first, in May 1943.

Other Residences

George and Martha Washington's Mount Vernon estate extended over 8,000 acres and was divided into five farms. Each farm was a complete unit with its own overseers, workforce of slaves, livestock, equipment, and buildings.

Montpelier was the lifelong home of James Madison, who described the Piedmont, Virginia, mansion and its grounds as just "a squirrel's jump from Heaven." The mansion remained in the family for three generations, from 1723 to 1844, beginning when

Ambrose Madison, the president's grandfather, was deeded the land until the widow Dolley Madison sold the estate.

Andrew Jackson's home in Nashville, Tennessee, was called The Hermitage, a residence on a working farm. The luxurious French silk wallpaper in the parlor suggested that its owner was well-off.

In 1865 after the Civil War, a small group of local Republicans who came to Illinois purchased a brick mansion for General Ulysses S. Grant for $2,500.

The Lincoln Log Cabin State Historic Site, eight miles south of Charleston, Illinois, preserves the last home of Abraham Lincoln's father and  stepmother, Thomas and Sarah Bush Lincoln. The 86-acre site, which includes the recon-structed Lincoln cabin and a surrounding farm, is managed by the Illinois Historic Preservation Agency.

After leaving the presidency, James Buchanan retired to his Georgian-style mansion in Pennsylvania, where he liked to entertain. The lavish house, called Wheatland, occupied four landscaped acres and contained a smokehouse and a privy.

Both Franklin D. Roosevelt and Eleanor Roosevelt had cottages in New York State, where they entertained intimate groups of friends and escaped the pressures of public life. Franklin's was Top Cottage, a small structure built on the grounds of his Springwood estate. Eleanor's was Val-Kill Cottage in the Hudson River Valley.

Barboursville, the former Palladian mansion of Senator James Barbour, is one of five Virginia houses designed by Thomas Jefferson. Another is Poplar Forest, an octagonal brick house that sits within a white-fenced octagonal plot of land.

The Alabama house of James Monroe, Oak Hill, was designed by Thomas Jefferson. Monroe retired there, but later lost the house to his creditors.

Theodore Roosevelt's Summer White House at Sagamore Hill in Oyster Bay, New York, remained in the family from 1885 until Roosevelt's death in 1919. From 1902 to 1908, the gray-shingled house was the locale of important presidential decisions.

President James Tyler's Sherwood Forest plantation, constructed in 1720, is a classic example of Virginia Tidewater design, featuring a huge house, little house, colonnade, and kitchen. Tyler bought the plantation from his cousin, Collier Minge, while he was still in the White House and renamed the plantation Sherwood Forest, referring to his reputation as a political outlaw. The estate has been the continuous residence of the James Tyler family since the president bought it in 1842. With a length of 300 feet, it is known to be the longest frame house in America.

Florida's only presidential museum is found in Key West. In 1890 it served as the first officer's quarters on a naval station. After the structure was converted into a private home, the inventor Thomas Edison

lived there. In 1946, President Harry S. Truman began
visiting the island for rest and relaxation. He spent so
much time there that reporters began to call it the
Little White House.

Richard Nixon and his friend, Jackie Gleason, star of
the television show *The Honeymooners*, played on
Gleason's golf course. Nixon's nearby Key Biscayne,
Florida, estate was dubbed "the Winter White House"
during the Nixon presidency. The U.S. Army Corps
built a helipad on the property for the president. The
contemporary 1.6-acre estate, with views of the
Miami skyline, had a four-car garage, six bedrooms,
and eight baths.

Monticello
Jefferson's mansion in Virginia, Monticello ("Little
Hill"), was based on Italian-influenced Palladian
architecture. The mansion featured many of
Jefferson's scientific inventions, including the first
revolving door. Approached from the front, Monticello
appears to be a one-story villa. The lower floor is
disguised in the hillside. The floor of the entry room

of Monticello is painted green. Jefferson wanted guests to feel as if they were still outside upon entering the house.

How grand is Jefferson's Monticello? The first design of Monticello had 14 rooms. Later renovations brought the total up to 43 rooms—33 in the main house, four in the adjacent pavilions, and six under the south terrace. (The stable and carriage bays under the north terrace were not included in these totals.) The living area in the main house is about 11,000 square feet, including the cellars below the house. There are 13 skylights, including the oculus under the main dome, and the walls vary in thickness from 13 to 27 inches. Eight fireplaces grace the main floor of the house as well as two openings for stoves. Today about one-third of the window glass in the mansion is original.

Monticello appears on the reverse side of the nickel.

Western White Houses

The Western White House is the name for various presidential residences, other than the White House, used for official government business. These homes have been located in the Midwestern and Western regions of the United States. During World War II, Franklin D. Roosevelt administered the duties of his office from the Royal Hawaiian Hotel in Honolulu, Hawaii. Richard Nixon conducted government business from La Casa Pacifica in San Clemente, California, and Ronald Reagan from Rancho del Cielo in Santa Barbara County in California. George W. Bush managed presidential duties from Prairie Chapel Ranch in Texas. All these homes have been called the Western White House when an active president was in residence.

In 1969, President Richard Nixon bought a beachfront mansion in San Clemente, California, with 21 acres of land. The house, named La Casa Pacifica, was over 6,000 square feet and had a heliport. Nixon also bought land adjacent to the estate for security. After Nixon resigned from the presidency in 1974, he and his wife, Patricia Nixon, returned to La Casa Pacifica, where they lived until they sold it and moved to New York City in 1980.

The Secret Service code name for Nixon's mansion in San Clemente, California, was Storm King, because it sat close to the ocean, resembled a huge World War II troop and cargo ship of that name, and was a subject of controversy in its being financed in part with federal funds.

In 1992, the CIA uncovered a bizarre Cuban plot to place President Nixon's Winter White House at Key Biscayne under surveillance. The plan called for ugging the Nixon residence, followed by a commando raid by Cuban frogmen.

Ronald Reagan spent nearly one-eighth of his presidency at his Western White House, Rancho del Cielo ("Ranch in the Sky") in Santa Barbara County, California. Ronald and Nancy Reagan bought the 688-acre ranch overlooking the Santa Ynez Valley and Pacific Ocean in 1974, shortly before Reagan completed his second term as governor of California.

Chapter 8
Presidential Sports and Hobbies

In the succession of presidents, we find the great divide: athletes like Ronald Reagan alongside bespectacled paper-scratchers like Calvin Coolidge. Then we have the worrisome, fretting Teddy Roosevelt who tried to ban football on college campuses to keep broken noses from interfering with studies. Nevertheless, presidents, for the most part, enjoyed some active leisure time. Even George Washington played a mean game of Rounders now and then.

Baseball

America's presidents have for a long time shown a keen interest in playing or watching a good game of baseball. A soldier's diary describes how George Washington and his men played an early version of baseball, called Rounders, on the fields of Valley Forge.

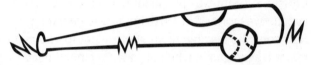

Historical records note that John Adams played a game called Bat and Ball.

Andrew Jackson played a baseball game called One Old Cat.

It was well known that Abraham Lincoln loved baseball. One historian notes that Lincoln kept a baseball in his desk "just in case there may be a two-minute hole in his schedule for a game of catch."

Andrew Johnson, Lincoln's successor, was invited to see the first game ever played between teams from different states. Johnson was so excited that he gave his White House staff time off from work to attend the game.

Ulysses S. Grant was president when the National League was formed in 1876, but it was Benjamin Harrison who became the first president to attend a major league game, when he saw Cincinnati beat Washington 7 to 4 on June 6, 1892.

In 1910, baseball was not very popular. To lure fans back into the ballpark and renew enthusiasm for the game, Clark Griffith, owner of the Washington Senators baseball team, invited President William McKinley to throw the first pitch at the opening game

between Washington and Brooklyn. McKinley agreed and the presidential box was erected. Although members of Congress filled the stands, McKinley never appeared. Nevertheless, the presence of important Congressmen boosted publicity for the ailing game, and attendance at games began to increase.

Although a gold season pass was issued to his successor, Teddy Roosevelt, he showed little interest in baseball.

Ronald Reagan loved baseball. His first career choice was as a radio announcer at WHO radio in Des Moines, Iowa, for the Chicago Cubs. He soon pursued acting and later starred in a baseball movie, *The Winning Team*.

Franklin D. Roosevelt was a big baseball fan. He knew how important the game was to Americans. During World War II, Roosevelt encouraged the Major Leagues to continue playing ball. He knew that continuing this popular pastime during the war would help boost the spirits of the American people.

Woodrow Wilson turned a few heads and caused a slight scandal when he brought a date to a World Series game. She was Edith Gault. This was the first time the couple had been seen in public since announcing their engagement. The next spring, he threw out the first pitch on opening day with the new Mrs. Wilson at his side.

"Good ballplayers make good citizens."—Chester A. Arthur

John F. Kennedy's father, Joseph, was able to convince a London paper to carry American baseball scores so that the Kennedys could read the news abroad.

John F. Kennedy loved sports, particularly baseball. He was an avid fan of his hometown Boston Red Sox team, but he never had a chance to attend any of their games while president. He was well known for his official appointment of a scorekeeper and stat advisor which he affectionately titled Undersecretary of Baseball.

Stan Musial of the St. Louis Cardinals openly campaigned for, financially supported, and verbally endorsed the John F. Kennedy–Lyndon B. Johnson ticket. Musial was elected sportsman of the decade for 1946 to 1956. He was also admitted to the Baseball Hall of Fame.

John F. Kennedy said, in a conversation with baseball star Stan Musial at a St. Louis Cardinals game in 1962: "A couple of years ago, they told me I was too young to be president and you were too old to be playing baseball. But we fooled them."

John F. Kennedy also said: "Last year, more Americans went to symphonies than went to baseball games. This may be viewed as an alarming statistic, but I think that both baseball and the country will endure."

At the 1962 season opener, Willie Tasby of the Baltimore Orioles hit a pop fly that headed straight for the head of President John F. Kennedy. Dave Powers, a cabinet member, courageously stood up to intercept the ball that was then deflected from its course, and the president was safe.

President John F. Kennedy autographed a baseball for Jim Rivera of the Chicago White Sox. Reacting to the illegible autograph, Rivera joked: "What kind of garbage college is that Harvard, where they don't even teach you to write? Do you think I can go into any tavern on Chicago's South Side and really say the president of the United States signed this baseball for me? I'd be run off. Take this thing back and give me something besides your garbage autograph." Kennedy good-naturedly took the ball back and carefully wrote his name on it before giving it back. Rivera replied, "You know, you're all right!"

When he attended ball games, Richard Nixon normally watched the games from the stands—like the average fan—rather than from a luxury box, the dugout, or sidelines. Major League Baseball celebrated its centennial in 1969. The afternoon before the game, President Nixon held a reception at the White House for the players and their wives. At this gathering, Baseball Commissioner Bowie Kuhn gave the president a trophy that read: "Baseball's Number One Fan."

George H. W. Bush was the captain of his baseball team at Yale University.

George W. Bush, former co-owner of the Texas Rangers baseball team, has a collection of over 250 signed baseballs.

Football

Believing it too dangerous, President Theodore Roosevelt tried to ban the game of football. As a result of witnessing many football injuries, Roosevelt was responsible for requiring protective gear—the helmets and pads that are now standard.

A handful of presidents played college football, including Dwight D. Eisenhower at West Point, Gerald Ford at the University of Michigan, John F. Kennedy at Harvard, Richard Nixon at Whittier College, and Ronald Reagan at Eureka College.

Jimmy Carter played football recreationally at the Naval Academy.

Gerald Ford was an assistant football coach when attending law school at Yale.

Ronald Reagan was so nearsighted that, as a college football player, his vision was limited to the area in front of him, occupied by the opposing team's player.

John F. Kennedy played football for both Choate and Harvard, but he never lettered in the sport.

Richard Nixon was a running back for Whittier College.

After numerous knee injuries, Dwight D. Eisenhower was forced to abandon football at West Point.

As head coach of the Wesleyan College football team in Connecticut from 1888 to 1890, Woodrow Wilson never experienced a losing season.

While a student at Stanford University, Herbert Hoover was hired to collect the stadium receipts for the football games. On one occasion, the half-time guest speaker was President Benjamin Harrison. He entered the event without paying, whereupon Hoover confronted him and demanded the twenty-five-cent admission. The stunned, but amused, Harrison complied.

President Reagan not only played football in high school and college, he also portrayed Notre Dame football legend George Gipp in the 1940 film *Knute Rockne, All American*. The role earned Reagan the nickname, "The Gipper," which stayed with him throughout his career.

When in office, the Reagans were avid football fans. Ronald Reagan went to the airport to congratulate the Redskins upon their return to Washington, D.C., after winning the Super Bowl in 1983.

Andrew Jackson was born in Waxaw County, on the border between North Carolina and South Carolina, but the exact location of his birth remains a mystery. Over the years both states claimed the president's birthright. After numerous unsettled disputes, the residents of both states resorted to a friendly football competition to decide the matter. This established a tradition. Each year they play football, and award a trophy bust of Jackson that's displayed at the victor's courthouse until the next game.

President John F. Kennedy said: "Politics is an astonishing profession. It has enabled me to go from being an obscure member of junior varsity at Harvard to being an honorary member of the Football Hall of Fame."

When growing up or at family gatherings, John F. Kennedy often played football with his brothers on

the lawn of the Kennedy estate in Hyannisport,
Massachusetts.

In the Swim

During his presidency, John Quincy Adams began
many mornings by swimming nude in the cold
Potomac River. A special fenced beach was
constructed so that the president could enjoy his
privacy.

Although confined to a wheelchair, Franklin D.
Roosevelt enjoyed fishing and sailing. Swimming
was a favorite part of his exercise regimen. In 1933,
Roosevelt had an indoor pool built in the White
House to enable him to continue swimming
throughout the year.

President Lyndon B. Johnson also enjoyed a swim.
However, he often turned his swim in the White
House pool or in the pool at his ranch into a political
conference. He even encouraged some aides to put
down their notebooks and enjoy a dip before lunch.

Golf

In the 20th century, only three presidents were not golfers—Herbert Hoover, Harry S. Truman, and Jimmy Carter. Although Lyndon B. Johnson played, he was reportedly bored by golf. Someone said that his golf club struck the ball as though he were killing a rattlesnake.

After the Watergate disclosures, Richard Nixon turned to golf. "Golf became my lifesaver," he said. The game offered him some exercise and the companionship of close friends.

Gerald Ford said that presidents are competitive by nature. On the golf course, they can aggressively pursue victory without worrying about offending a foreign dignitary or prominent political ally. Gerald Ford sometimes hit spectators with badly aimed drives.

Woodrow Wilson, who played golf as frequently as six times a week in every sort of weather, dismissed the notion that his love for the sport could cause him political problems. He was on the course when word arrived in 1915 that a German submarine had sunk the passenger liner *Lusitania*. He headed to his country club just one day after asking Congress to declare war on Germany.

Before polio disabled him, Franklin D. Roosevelt enjoyed golf. Through the Public Works Administration, as part of Roosevelt's New Deal, he launched programs to help lift the country out of the Depression. More than 250 public golf courses were built.

Lyndon B. Johnson refused to let the public see him playing golf during the Vietnam War, believing it unseemly in light of the combat deaths of soldiers.

On August 4, 2002, George W. Bush, speaking to the press during a round of golf at his retreat in Kennebunkport, Maine, declared: "I call upon all nations to do everything they can to stop these terrorist killers. Thank you. Now watch this drive."

The United States Golf Association honored the cheerful Warren G. Harding by naming the U.S. Public Links Championship trophy after him. Harding, in spite of Prohibition, enjoyed a scotch-and-soda after playing four holes.

So many Secret Service agents went with Dwight D. Eisenhower on his numerous rounds (most carrying golf bags filled with high-powered rifles) that comedian Bob Hope joked that with so many people watching, he had trouble cheating.

Eisenhower may have had more impact on golf than any other president. He frequently carried a golf club as he walked through the White House, and he transformed the South Lawn into a practice facility for hitting long irons. Along with Arnold Palmer, Eisenhower helped start the big golf boom of the 1950s and 1960s.

George H. W. Bush paid a price for defending his right to play golf in wartime. When the Gulf War erupted in 1991, Bush stated that he refused to be a prisoner in the White House and would continue to play golf. He quickly rescinded his statement after receiving heavy public criticism.

Golf-playing presidents have added colorful lore to the game. Legend has it that Calvin Coolidge, known for being tight with money, purposely hit only short shots so he would not lose any golf balls.

Lyndon B. Johnson made an art out of taking Mulligans (free extra shots). Usually only one is allowed per game, but Johnson stretched the rules.

George H. W. Bush took pride in playing 18 holes in under three hours, and Bill Clinton worked his way about a course in a leisurely five hours, laughing, joking, and hitting extra balls all the way.

To avoid crowds, John F. Kennedy, who reportedly possessed the most fluid of all presidential swings, usually started somewhere in the middle of the golf course and then jumped to adjoining holes.

Other Sports, Hobbies, and Games

"Walking is the best possible exercise. Habituate yourself to walk very far."—Thomas Jefferson

Gerald Ford was the only president to have been an All-American athlete in college. He enjoyed jogging, sailing, tennis, swimming, skiing, and shooting. He played golf in professional tournaments for charity and was in excellent physical shape when becoming president in 1962.

Herbert Hoover was a great advocate of the medicine ball to build strength and endurance. The heavy ball would be heaved about as a means of building strength and endurance. Hoover invited his cabinet and advisors to join him in an early morning ball-catching routine before breakfast. The group became known as the "medicine-ball cabinet."

Calvin Coolidge enjoyed golf, fishing, and trap shooting (shooting at clay pigeons with a shotgun). For exercise, he rode a mechanical horse and pitched hay. Coolidge also exercised with Indian clubs, a form of exercise very popular at the time.

Harry S. Truman enjoyed fishing, playing the piano, and walking. His daily walks, often accompanied by reporters, were conducted at a brisk pace of 120 paces per minute. Truman's walks continued long after he had left the White House. His walks were sometimes directed toward a place where he could "strike a blow for liberty" (have a drink).

Dwight D. Eisenhower enjoyed fishing, golfing, and hunting. Eisenhower was also talented at painting. A studio was set up in the White House to allow him to pursue his hobby.

Lyndon B. Johnson enjoyed the activities typical of a boy raised on a farm, such as fishing, hunting, and riding. Johnson tried to escape the pressures of the

Vietnam War by retreating to his Texas ranch, where he could indulge in these pastimes.

Jimmy Carter enjoyed jogging, swimming, skiing, canoeing, and fishing. He also played softball and tennis.

Ronald Reagan, our oldest president, enjoyed riding his horse at his ranch in California. Fancying himself as a true outdoorsman, he also chopped wood.

George H. W. Bush brought the game of horse shoes to the White House. He even had a horse-shoe court installed on the White House lawn. After leaving the White House, Bush took a well-publicized parachute jump to demonstrate his interest in skydiving.

While president, Theodore Roosevelt suffered a detached retina in a boxing match with an army officer. As a result of the injury, he became blind in one eye.

The teddy bear was named after President Theodore Roosevelt. While on a 1902 hunting trip in the

Mississippi Delta, Roosevelt refused to shoot a bear cub. Clifford Berryman's cartoon in *The Washington Star*, "Drawing the Line at Mississippi," showed Roosevelt with his back turned, refusing to shoot a small, large-eared bear roped by an aide. Inspired by "Teddy's bear," toymakers, who created stuffed bears, soon began to call them teddy bears.

President Richard Nixon took up bowling while he was president and could often be found in the White House bowling alley. The White House staff made efforts to publicize his hobby, staging photo opportunities, presenting Nixon as a regular individual with interests that he shared with many other Americans. Nixon always wanted to look like "one of the guys."

Richard Nixon said, "I like the job I have, but if I had to live my life over again, I would like to have ended up a sports writer."

Card-Playing Presidents

Harry S. Truman was playing poker when he found out that he would become president.

Dwight D. Eisenhower played bridge.

Richard Nixon became known as one of the best poker players in the Navy.

When Warren G. Harding was president, almost nightly poker games took place in the White House. Liquor was served during those games even during Prohibition. During his administration, many important deals were concluded during poker games. These included the transfer of oil reserve lands from the Department of the Navy to the Department of the Interior—the beginning of the infamous Teapot Dome scandal.

Chapter 9
Presidential Monuments and Memorials

The pharaohs have their pyramids, and America's presidents have their marble cakes—at least that's how one French diplomat described the architecture of Washington, D.C., in the 1800s. But who could imagine that city without Lincoln's rotunda or Washington's obelisk? A bit farther northwest, where else in the world can you see the monumental portraits of four great presidents carved into the side of a mountain? When a president leaves our country better off than he found it, we tend to remember him in a grand way.

George Washington has a bridge, a state, and a city named after him. Thirty states have counties named after George Washington.

The state of Colorado was originally called Jefferson in honor of Thomas Jefferson.

Four state capitals—Jackson, Mississippi; Lincoln, Nebraska; Jefferson City, Missouri; and Madison, Wisconsin—are named after presidents.

The faces of four presidents—Thomas Jefferson, Abraham Lincoln, Theodore Roosevelt, and George Washington—are carved into Mount Rushmore National Memorial in South Dakota.

The capital of Liberia, Monrovia, was named after James Monroe. Founded in 1822 during the term of President James Monroe, Monrovia was established by the American Colonization Society as a haven for freed slaves from the United States who wanted to return to Africa. The country was originally called Monrovia, but changed its name to the "Free and Independent Republic of Liberia" in 1847.

Franklin Pierce has a college named after him in New Hampshire.

The town of Lincoln, Illinois, was named for Abraham Lincoln in 1853.

Several mountains are named after presidents: Mount Adams in New Hampshire and Washington state; Mount Jefferson in Oregon; Mount Lincoln in Colorado; Mount Madison and Mount Washington in New Hampshire; Mount Grant in Nevada; and Mount Kennedy in Canada near the Alaskan border.

The Madison River in Montana was named for James Madison.

William Howard Taft was the first president to be buried in Arlington National Cemetery in Virginia.

In 1920, an Austrian astronomer discovered an asteroid and named it *Hooveria* in honor of Herbert Hoover. This was the first time an astronomical phenomenon was given such a moniker. The astronomer wanted to honor Hoover "as a man who worked hard in feeding hungry peoples left destitute by the planet Earth's most terrible war."

In the 19th century, botanists named two newly discovered palm trees after George Washington: the *Washingtonia filifera* (California fan palm) and the *Washingtonia robusta* (Mexican fan palm). Both belong to the botanical family *Washingtonia arecaceae*.

Botanists also named two species of plants after Thomas Jefferson: the *Jeffersonia diphylla* (twin leaf) and *Jeffersonia dubia* (white petal).

You can travel on the Lincoln Highway coast-to-coast. Begun in 1913, the Lincoln Highway was the first transcontinental highway constructed in the United States. Carl G. Fisher, an automotive industry pioneer, wanted to name it "Coast-to-Coast Rock Highway." But instead the highway was named after Lincoln. Beginning in the late 1920s, when numbered highways became the norm, most of the old Lincoln Highway became U.S. Highway 30.

The National Archives and Records Administration (NARA) supervises the presidential libraries, which hold the records of our nation's highest office. Together, these libraries house more than 400 million pages of letters, diaries, speeches, memos, and other documents, as well as photographs, film, audiotape, and even e-mails.

The Ronald Reagan Library has the distinction of having a retired *Air Force One* parked on its front lawn. The *Boeing 707* was pulled from service in September 2001 after flying for twenty-eight years. It had carried seven presidents since Richard Nixon, but Reagan logged more miles on it than any of his predecessors.

John F. Kennedy's passion for the sea was legendary, and perhaps no single item better represented that passion than his beloved sailboat, *Victura*, which now stands on the lawn of the Kennedy Library in Boston, Massachusetts.

The Lincoln Center for the Performing Arts (Lincoln Center) is a 15-acre complex of buildings in New York City. Named after our 16th president to honor a man who loved culture and learning, Lincoln Center was constructed during the 1960s and houses twelve major arts organizations.

The John F. Kennedy Center for the Performing Arts (Kennedy Center) opened in 1971 as a living memorial to John F. Kennedy. The idea for the center, however, dates to 1958, when a National Cultural Center was proposed for Washington, D.C. Designed by architect Edward Durrell Stone, the Kennedy Center is located on the Potomac River, adjacent to the Watergate Hotel.

The Franklin Delano Roosevelt Memorial is one of the newest memorials in Washington, D.C. Dedicated on May 2, 1997, the memorial traces the 12-year period during which FDR served as president. Each outdoor room is devoted to one of FDR's four terms in office. A 10-foot statue showing Roosevelt seated was considered controversial when disabled

Americans wanted to make his wheelchair more prominent.

The Jimmy Carter Library and Museum in Atlanta, Georgia, was built on land that had been acquired by the State of Georgia for a highway project that was canceled by Carter when he had been governor of Georgia. Construction started on October 2, 1984, and the library was opened to the public on Carter's 62nd birthday, October 1, 1986. The federal government owns and administers some parts of the complex, while other parts are privately owned and operated, including Carter's offices and the offices of the Carter Center, a nonprofit human rights agency. The Library has hosted special exhibits such as a showing of the United States Bill of Rights and Carter's Nobel Peace Prize.

The William J. Clinton Presidential Center in Little Rock, Arkansas, is the largest presidential library and one of the most dramatic. Designed by architect James Polshek, it cantilevers over the Arkansas River, echoing Clinton's famous campaign promise of "building a bridge to the 21st century." The archives hold 2 million photographs, 80 million pages of documents, 21 million e-mail messages, and nearly 80,000 artifacts from the Clinton presidency.

Is it Cape Canaveral or Cape Kennedy? Cape Canaveral, a strip of land in Florida near the Atlantic coast, is the site of the Kennedy Space Center and the Cape Canaveral Air Force Station. Most U.S. spacecraft are launched from either one of these sites. From 1963 to 1973 it was called Cape Kennedy in honor of John F. Kennedy, who enthusiastically supported and funded the space program. After his assassination in 1963, his widow, Jacqueline Kennedy, suggested that President Lyndon B. Johnson rename the Cape Canaveral facility Cape Kennedy.

Although the Interior Department approved this name change in 1964, it was not popular in Florida. In 1973, the Florida legislature passed a law restoring the former name. The Kennedy family issued a letter stating they "understood the decision."

The Massachusetts Institute of Technology's Lincoln Laboratory, also known as the Lincoln Lab, was founded to develop and advance electronics in the air defense systems of the United States. Funded by the Department of Defense, its mission is to apply science and advanced technology to solve critical problems of national security.

The Ronald Reagan Presidential Library in California houses over 50 million pages of government records as well as a large collection of photographs and film. Contents include an assortment of Reagan memorabilia from both his presidency and his term as governor of California, including a chunk of the Berlin Wall. The Reagan library was the largest presidential library until the William J. Clinton Presidential Center opened in Little Rock, Arkansas.

The *U.S.S. Jimmy Carter* (SSN–23), the third and last Seawolf-class submarine, is the only ship of the United States Navy to be named in honor of a former president. Jimmy Carter, a nuclear engineer, served as an officer in the Navy.

The Jefferson National Expansion Memorial consists of a 90-acre park along the Mississippi River in Saint Louis, Missouri. Because it sits near the starting point of the Lewis and Clark Expedition, the memorial commemorates the Louisiana Purchase and settlement of the American West. The park also contains the famous Gateway Arch that symbolizes the city.

Notable Memorials and Monuments

Monument or memorial—what's the difference? A single structure or series of structures honoring a president may be referred to as either a monument or a memorial.

Memorials are intended to help us remember people who have passed away.

Monuments are large architectural structures. Ships, bridges, parks, tunnels, and cities named after presidents memorialize their names. So do geological formations and even botanical discoveries—as the name *Washingtonia arecaceae* (plant genus + species) demonstrates.

Mount Rushmore

Located in Keystone, South Dakota, the Mount Rushmore National Memorial Park was created to represent the first 150 years of American history. Between 1927 and 1941, sculptor Gutzon Borglum and 400 workers created the 60-foot busts of Presidents George Washington, Thomas Jefferson, Theodore Roosevelt, and Abraham Lincoln. The park spreads across 1,278 acres and was designated a national memorial on March 3, 1925.

On July 4, 2005, Alfred Kaercher, a German manufacturer of cleaning machines, started the 3-week process of cleaning the faces on Mount Rushmore to remove lichen, algae, moss, and other organic stains that could damage the underlying rock through bio-corrosion. The washing was completed in August.

The rock formation is carved on a sacred Lakota site. In tribute to the Native American tribe and its chief, another sculptor has been constructing the Crazy Horse Memorial out of a rock face in the Black Hills of South Dakota, just 17 miles from Mount Rushmore.

The Strange History of the Lincoln Memorial

In 1900 the tomb of Abraham Lincoln, assassinated in 1865, had to be rebuilt. The Great Emancipator, as he was known, had to be moved to a temporary grave to foil potential grave robbers. Lincoln's body was put inside a cage and covered with concrete until a permanent site could be found. Draining the swampland that became the home of the Lincoln Memorial began in 1901.

The first stone was put into place on Lincoln's birthday, February 12, 1915. After completion, President Warren G. Harding dedicated the memorial on May 30, 1922. Lincoln's only surviving child, Robert Todd Lincoln, attended the dedication. The monument's sculptor, Daniel Chester French, chose to seat Lincoln and portray him as

worn and pensive, gazing eastward to the Washington Monument. One hand is clenched, the other open. Because French had a hearing-impaired daughter, the hands purportedly represent the letters "A" and "L" in American Sign Language. Others have read determination in the closed fist and openness in the more open hand. The Piccirilli Brothers carved the statue from 28 blocks of Georgia marble.

The Washington Monument

At just over 555 feet (169 meters), the Washington Monument is considered to be the tallest piece of freestanding masonry in the world. The obelisk (needle) is modeled after ancient Egyptian artifacts, quite popular with architects in Europe and the United States in the 19th century.

After Washington left office, Congress considered the construction of a monument to honor the first U.S. president. By 1847, $87,000 had been collected in part by public subscription. The remaining funds came from federal sources. The construction of the Washington Monument began in 1848 and was not completed until 1884, almost 30 years after architect Robert Mills's death. Lack of funds and the Civil War interrupted the work. A difference in shading of the marble (visible approximately 150 feet up) clearly delineates the first phase of construction from its last phase in 1876.

The Washington Monument was originally designed with a Greek Doric-style rotunda at the base of the obelisk. Lack of funding necessitated the more austere design we know today. It is composed of marble, granite, and sandstone.

When it was completed and dedicated in 1888, at 155 feet (169 m), the Washington monument became the world's tallest structure. It held this title for just one year, until 1889 when the Eiffel Tower was completed in Paris, France, for the Universal Exposition (World's Fair).

The present elevator of the Washington Monument was installed in 1988 and takes 60 seconds to travel to the top. The monument's stairwell contains 896 steps.

The Jefferson Memorial

In 1934 Congress passed a resolution to create a memorial commemorating Thomas Jefferson. It was designed by John Russell Pope, the architect of the original building of the National Gallery of Art. The Jefferson Memorial was officially dedicated on April 13, 1943, the 200th anniversary of Jefferson's birth.

In designing the Jefferson Memorial, architect John Russell Pope wished to echo the Palladian style of buildings designed by Jefferson, such as his beloved Monticello. The Monument was criticized in the press as "rehashed classicism, dead to the eye."

The Jefferson Memorial features a 19-foot 10,000-pound (5.7-m 4,500-kg) bronze statue of Jefferson by sculptor Rudolph Evans, which was added four years after the dedication. The interior walls are engraved with passages from Jefferson's writings, including the prominent, "I have sworn upon the altar of God eternal hostility against every form of tyranny over the mind of man," taken from a letter by Jefferson to Dr. Benjamin Rush.

Grant's Tomb

Who's Buried in Grant's Tomb? Ulysses S. Grant is buried near the intersection of Riverside Drive and 122nd Street in New York City. The mausoleum contains the body of Grant and his wife, Julia Dent Grant. Designed by architect John Duncan, the granite and marble structure was completed in 1897 and was the largest mausoleum in North America at the time. A huge public subscription paid for it.

Sculptor Henry Mervin Shrady spent 20 years building the General Grant National Memorial. Shrady paid particular attention to portraying Grant with a look of calmness and control to reflect Grant's reputation as a coolheaded military leader.

Chapter 10
Presidential Oddities

Some of the most influential presidents came to the office by way, it seems, of a string of odd jobs and personal eccentricities. Maybe Calvin Coolidge forged his business philosophy while assembling dolls in Massachusetts or Grover Cleveland his politics while a sheriff in New York. And what can we possibly say about Ronald Reagan's obsession with jelly beans? Nevertheless, Americans seem to enjoy the quirks of their chief executive—especially when quirky behavior is caught on tape and aired on the evening news.

Ulysses S. Grant smoked about 20 cigars per day. Not surprisingly, he died of throat cancer.

Calmed only by brandy, James Polk survived gall-bladder surgery at the age of 17.

Presidents George Washington, Thomas Jefferson, James Madison, James Monroe, William Henry Harrison, John Tyler, Zachary Taylor, and Woodrow Wilson were all born in Virginia. This state produced more presidents than any other.

Presidents Ulysses S. Grant, Rutherford B. Hayes, James Garfield, Benjamin Harrison, William McKinley, William Howard Taft, and Warren G. Harding were all born in Ohio.

Calvin Coolidge, suffering from chronic stomach pain, required 10 to 11 hours of sleep and an afternoon nap every day.

Zachary Taylor's horse grazed on the White House lawn.

Presidents George Washington, Thomas Jefferson, James Madison, Andrew Jackson, James Polk, and Zachary Taylor had owned slaves.

Presidents George Washington, Thomas Jefferson, Martin Van Buren, Andrew Jackson, Ulysses S. Grant, Calvin Coolidge, and Dwight D. Eisenhower had red hair in their youth. Of course, some wore a wig, were bald, or had gray or white hair when they took office.

Before he became president, Grover Cleveland worked as a sheriff.

Calvin Coolidge had once been a toy maker.

Because he was known to love the high life, fine clothes, and high society, Chester A. Arthur was known as Gentleman Boss and Elegant Arthur.

William Henry Harrison's campaign slogan was "Tippecanoe and Tyler, Too." He was the hero of the battle of Tippecanoe, and John Tyler was his running mate. Not even in office for one month, Harrison caught pneumonia and died on April 4, 1841. He was the first president to die in office. The second president to die in office was Zachary Taylor, who was also a general. He was the last Whig to be elected president.

Until he was five years old, Franklin D. Roosevelt's mother had her son wear a dress. In the late 19th century little preschool boys commonly wore dresses.

John Adams was elected as vice president to George Washington and took the oath on April 21, 1789. This was nine days before George Washington took the oath, on April 30th.

Frederick the Great was so impressed with George Washington's talent for always turning near defeat into victories that the king sent the general a sword with the inscription: "From the oldest general in the world, to the best."

Two presidents, George Washington and James Garfield, are thought to have died at the hands of incompetent physicians. George Washington died from loss of blood. As a common treatment for "inflammatory quinsy," his physicians bled him several times, yielding about 5 pints (2.75 liters) of blood in less than 16 hours. Modern physicians, however, consider that Washington may have died of acute bacterial epiglottitis.

James Garfield died when doctors probed and contaminated his bullet wound with unsterilized fingers. One finger, searching for the bullet, even punctured his liver. Alexander Graham Bell was called in to help locate the bullet but failed. Garfield died from the infection resulting from all these probes. His assassin was Charles Guiteau, who was disappointed and enraged that Garfield would not appoint him as U.S. consul in Paris.

To satisfy the curiosity of modern historians, on June 17, 1991, Zachary Taylor's body was exhumed and tested to determine if he was poisoned. No traces of poison were found.

William Howard Taft was America's largest president, tipping the scales at over 300 pounds (135 kg). The bathtub in his New York City home was custom made at 8 x 5 feet (2.4 x 1.5 m). He reportedly got stuck in the White House bathtub, and it took four men to pull him loose.

Abraham Lincoln talked so much in his sleep that guards sometimes entered his room to check to see if he was alone.

During his presidency, Theodore Roosevelt lost partial sight in one eye as the result of a boxing match. His sparring partner was a young army captain.

Millard Fillmore had a stroke while shaving.

After a disfiguring cancer operation, President Grover Cleveland wore a prosthesis made of rubber to support his jawbone.

James Madison was an epileptic.

After Abraham Lincoln returned to Washington after delivering the Gettysburg Address, he contracted smallpox. Now that he had something to give that no one wanted, he joked, "Where are the office seekers?"

Franklin D. Roosevelt suffered an attack of polio at age 39. The resulting paralysis was kept in low profile throughout his presidency. Roosevelt was usually photographed only from the waist up.

Theodore Roosevelt had Joseph Pulitzer and his *New York World* newspaper indicted for criminal libel after the newspaper charged, "corrupt promoters had made millions in connection with the digging of the Panama Canal." To avoid arrest, Pulitzer cruised offshore in his yacht, named *Liberty*. Ultimately the case was dismissed.

Only two U.S. presidents have been impeached (formally accused of imroper conduct): Andrew Johnson (by one vote) and Bill Clinton. Richard Nixon was not impeached; he resigned from the presidency.

The First and Second Continental Congress presidents and the "president of the United States, in Congress Assembled" were not technically presidents of the United States. They were presiding officers over the Continental Congress, which most resembles a legislative body. They were not members of a distinct executive branch like that of the presidency today. Seventeen different men served in this capacity between 1781 and 1788.

George Washington, John Adams, Thomas Jefferson, James Madison, James Monroe, John Quincy Adams, Andrew Jackson, and William Henry Harrison were born British subjects, since all were born in colonies belonging to the British Empire.

Due to an accident on his father's farm, John Quincy Adam's right arm was malformed and smaller than his left arm.

At his inauguration, George Washington had only one real tooth. At various times he wore dentures made of human or animal teeth, ivory, or lead, but never wood.

The six white horses in Washington's stables had their teeth brushed every morning on Washington's orders.

Washington's 183-word inauguration speech took just 90 seconds to read. A few historians speculate that it was hard for him to enunciate because of his false teeth.

At home in Mount Vernon, George Washington installed two ice-cream freezers.

Washington did not wear a powdered wig, considered high fashion in the late 1700s. Instead, he powdered his reddish-brown hair and tied it in a short braid down his back.

George Washington carried a portable sundial.

George Washington issued an order to the U.S. Army that forbade swearing.

Washington's I.Q. is estimated at about 125.

George Washington snored loudly. When in the field with the Continental Army, his snoring kept the guards on duty and others from falling asleep.

On his deathbed, Washington took his own pulse and noted the declining rate.

George Washington and Abraham Lincoln had large feet. Washington wore size thirteen boots and Lincoln wore size fourteen. Lincoln often complained that his feet were cold.

At age 70, Jefferson declared that he had never lost an (adult) tooth.

In 1841, a Louisville, Kentucky, dentist fractured Lincoln's jaw bone when attempting to extract a tooth, without anesthesia.

Abraham Lincoln talked so much in his sleep that guards sometimes entered his room to check to see if he was alone.

The new electric lights so frightened Benjamin Harrison and his wife that he had his White House staff turn them on and off. They feared being electrocuted.

A health-conscious Millard Fillmore didn't smoke or drink and took measures to avoid malaria.

Under instructions from Franklin Pierce, James Buchanan was ordered to "detach" Cuba from Spain.

John Adams had a forceful and commanding presence, although he was a small man.

When he was over 80 years old and had lost his teeth, John Adams spoke with difficulty.

President Ulysses S. Grant was tone deaf. As president, he was once asked if he liked the music he had just heard in a concert. "How could I? I know only two tunes. One of them is 'Yankee Doodle' and the other isn't."

After only thirty-two days in office, President William Henry Harrison died from pneumonia. He was thought to have contracted it during his inauguration ceremony held in March in bitter weather to which he wore no hat or coat.

President Benjamin Harrison, grandson of President William Henry Harrison, reportedly wore chamois under his suit as he took the oath of office. It was conducted in a rainstorm under a sea of umbrellas on the East Portico of the Capitol. Former President Cleveland held an umbrella over Harrison's head. Over 12,000 people attended inaugural balls.

Obsessed with germs, Benjamin Harrison wore gloves while shaking hands and was called the Human Iceberg.

Teddy Roosevelt was the ultimate long-winded speaker. On at least one occasion, it actually saved his life. At a campaign stop in Milwaukee in 1912, Roosevelt had a 50-page speech, folded in half, with a steel case for spectacles in his inside coat pocket. The thick paper and spectacle case blunted the force of a potential assassin's bullet. The bullet entered his chest on the right side and traveled 3 inches, missing his heart and any pleural cavity. The bullet remained lodged and apparently caused him little trouble.

William McKinley's handshake was famous. To save wear and tear on his right hand at receptions, the president developed what came to be called the "McKinley grip." In receiving lines, he would smile as a man came by, take his right hand and squeeze it warmly before his own hand got caught in a hard grip, hold the man's elbow with his left hand, and then swiftly pull him along and be ready to beam on the next guest.

Unlike James Polk and William McKinley, both of whom carefully studied the art of shaking hands, Woodrow Wilson's handshake was described as "a ten-cent pickled mackerel in brown paper."

Ronald Reagan had poor eyesight. Later in life, Reagan wore contact lenses. When delivering a speech he would remove one lens so that he could read his notes and leave one lens in so that he could see the audience. Those around Reagan commonly saw him reinserting a contact lens after speaking.

The annual White House reception, in which Herbert Hoover had to shake hands with thousands of visitors, was a problem. His hand was at times so swollen that he could not write for days. Once he received a bad cut from a diamond ring that was turned inward; the reception was abruptly halted. He did not believe in the "McKinley Grip."

Theodore Roosevelt did not allow visitors to smoke in the White House.

Woodrow Wilson, who may have had dyslexia that caused early difficulty, did not learn to read until he was about 10 years old in 1866. His father educated him despite disruptions during the Civil War. Wilson later compensated by teaching himself shorthand and overcame his disability, earning a Ph.D. from Johns Hopkins and later becoming president of Princeton University.

Woodrow Wilson had an annoying habit of busily polishing his eyeglasses while people were talking to him.

Wanting to drive a car although his legs were paralyzed, in 1936 Franklin D. Roosevelt had a Ford Deluxe Phaeton convertible equipped with hand controls for the clutch, brake, and throttle. This gave him independence by enabling him to drive around his estate and the surrounding countryside. The car is now on permanent display at the Roosevelt Library.

President Ronald Reagan kept a
large jar of jelly beans on his desk
and offered them to visitors. He
began eating jelly beans when he
stopped smoking in the 1960s.

In January 1992, while at a formal dinner in Japan,
George H. W. Bush became ill and threw up on the
lap of the Prime Minister of Japan, Miyazawa Kiichi.

The first e-mail message sent into space (not virtual
space!) was from President Bill Clinton to astronaut
John Glenn, while Glenn was orbiting the earth on
the space shuttle. Almost 40 million e-mail messages
were created during the Clinton Administration.

It Could Have Been July 2, 1776

On July 2, 1776, twelve of the Thirteen Colonies
officially became the United States of America. New
York held out. The next day, John Adams wrote to his
wife Abigail, "The second day of July 1776 will be the
most memorable epoch in the history of America...It
ought to be solemnized with pomp and parade, with

shows, games, sports, guns, bells, bonfires, and illuminations from one end of this continent to the other from this time forward forever more."

After debate and a few changes on July 3 and 4, the Continental Congress approved the Declaration of Independence, which was printed on a broadside in Philadelphia by John Dunlap the evening of July 4th.

Fifty-six people signed the Declaration of Independence. John Hancock signed it on July 4th. The remaining 52 members of Congress signed the Declaration on August 2nd when the official parchment version was finished. The remaining three members did not sign until much later. Thomas McKean of Delaware did not sign until 1781. Future Presidents John Adams and Thomas Jefferson were among the signatories.

In America, the signing of the Declaration of Independence was greeted as a major historical event. In England, the event was hardly noticed at all, not until August—the time it took for news to travel in those days. The news received only six lines on an inside page of a London paper.

Thomas Jefferson wrote the Declaration of Independence, but he didn't really feel he was the right person for the job. John Adams had a difficult time convincing Jefferson he was indeed the most qualified person for the task.

The Declaration of Independence was first publicly proclaimed on July 8th and read to George Washington and his troops in New York, where Washington was already fighting the British.

Chapter II
Presidential Quotes and Opinions

In Thomas Jefferson's day, the public read eloquent and thoughtful utterances from the man at the top. Today the most innocent gaffe out of the mouth of George W. Bush circulates around the world in minutes by e-mail. What are we to make of it? Only that presidents, like the rest of us, have some good ideas and some bad ones; some musings that should be boldly stated and others that should forever remain unspoken.

Since they have been retold decade after decade, spoken words supposedly from the mouths of presidents may have been altered somewhat in the retelling.

"He [Andrew Jackson] makes sad havoc of the King's English. The English are upset by the grammar, accent, rate, and clarity of American speech, but perhaps most of all by the misuse of English words. They do not appreciate the differences in accent and dialect as something uniquely American; rather, they see it as another inferiority to Great Britain."
—Thomas Hamilton, British ambassador

"No man is good enough to govern another man without that other's consent."—Abraham Lincoln, 1854

"Ozone Man, ozone. He's crazy, way out, far out, man."—George H. W. Bush, speaking about Al Gore during the 1992 presidential campaign

"A conservative is a man with two perfectly good legs who, however, has never learned how to walk forward."—Franklin D. Roosevelt

"One of the great things about this country [Iraq] is a lot of people pray."—George W. Bush, April 13, 2003

"It is not the critic who counts: not the man who points out how the strong man stumbles or where the doer of deeds could have done better. The credit belongs to the man who is actually in the arena, whose face is marred by dust and sweat and blood, who strives valiantly, who errs and comes up short again and again, because there is no effort without error or shortcoming, but who knows the great enthusiasms, the great devotions, who spends himself for a worthy cause; who, at the best, knows, in the end, the triumph of high achievement, and who, at the worst, if he fails, at least he fails while daring greatly, so that his place shall never be with those cold and timid souls who knew neither victory nor defeat."—Theodore Roosevelt, speech delivered in Paris, April 23, 1910

"The slogan 'Press on!' has solved and always will solve the problems of the human race."
—Calvin Coolidge

"Things may come to those who wait, but only the things left by those who hustle."—Abraham Lincoln

"You can fool all of the people some of the time, and some of the people all of the time, but you cannot fool all of the people all of the time."
—Abraham Lincoln

"'Tis better to remain silent and be thought a fool than to speak and remove all doubt."—Abraham Lincoln

"He can compress the most words into the smallest ideas of any man I ever met."—Abraham Lincoln

"Whenever I hear anyone arguing for slavery, I feel a strong impulse to see it tried on him personally."
—Abraham Lincoln

"I am not one who—who flamboyantly believes in throwing a lot of words around."—George H. W. Bush

"It was involuntary. They sank my boat."—John F. Kennedy, when asked how he became a war hero.

"I am not worried about the deficit. It is big enough to take care of itself."—Ronald Reagan

"Leave the matter of religion to the family altar, the church and the private school supported entirely by private contributions. Keep the church and state forever separate."—Ulysses S. Grant, Address to the Society of the Army of the Tennessee, given in Des Moines, Iowa, on September, 30, 1875

"Every man, conducting himself as a good citizen, and being accountable to God alone for his religious opinions, ought to be protected in worshipping the Deity according to the dictates of his own conscience."—George Washington

"Encourage free schools and resolve that not one dollar, appropriated for their support, shall be appropriated to the support of any sectarian schools."—Ulysses S. Grant, speech to the Society of the Army of the Tennessee in Des Moines, Iowa, September 30, 1875

"I would also like to call your attention to the importance of correcting an evil that, if allowed to continue, will probably lead to great trouble in our land before the close of the 19th century. It is the accumulation of vast amounts of untaxed church property."—Ulysses S. Grant, State of the Union address, December 7, 1875

"Blessed are the young, for they shall inherit the national debt."—Herbert Hoover

"The truth will set you free, but first it will make you miserable."—James A. Garfield

"A radical is a man with both feet planted firmly in the air."—Franklin D. Roosevelt

"The most valuable of all talents is never using two words when one will do."—Thomas Jefferson

"It ain't what they call you; it's what you answer to."—comedian W. C. Fields, quoted by Bill Clinton

"You do not lead by hitting people over the head. That's assault, not leadership."—Dwight D. Eisenhower

"They misunderestimated me."—George W. Bush, November 6, 2000 *Many people delighted in collecting Bush quotes with inappropriate or garbled words and phrases. He wasn't the first president to be guilty of assaults on the English language.*

"The President has kept all of the promises he intended to keep."—former Clinton aide, George Stephanopoulos, commenting on Bill Clinton on the television talk show, *Larry King Live*, 1996

"Just think how much you're going to be missing. You don't have Nixon to kick around anymore." —Richard Nixon after losing the 1962 California gubernatorial race to Pat Brown

"I've always thought and said farmers are the smartest people in the world. They don't go for high hats, and they can spot a phony a mile off." —Harry S. Truman

"In any moment of decision, the best thing you can do is the right thing, the next best thing is the wrong

thing, and the worst thing you can do is nothing."
—Theodore Roosevelt

"Sometimes one man with courage is a majority."
—Andrew Jackson

"Nearly all men can stand adversity, but if you want
to test a man's character, give him power."
—Abraham Lincoln

"Congress wouldn't act [to support faith-based
initiatives], so I signed an executive order. That
means I did it on my own."—George W. Bush,
March 3, 2003

"It's not me who can't keep a secret. It's the people I
tell that can't."—Abraham Lincoln

"I have wondered at times what the Ten
Commandments would have looked like if Moses
had run them through the U.S. Congress."
—Ronald Reagan

"You gave me the ride of my life, and I probably gave as good as I got."—Bill Clinton, bidding farewell to supporters when leaving the office of president, Washington, D.C., January 20, 2000

"I call upon all nations to do everything they can to stop these terrorist killers. Thank you. Now watch this drive."—George W. Bush, speaking to the press during a round of golf, Kennebunkport, Maine, August 4, 2002

"This is a great day for France!"—Richard Nixon, while attending Charles De Gaulle's funeral

"The caribou love it. They rub against it and they have babies. There are more caribou in Alaska than you can shake a stick at."—George H. W. Bush, about the Alaskan pipeline, 1991

"I hope I stand for anti-bigotry, anti-Semitism, anti-racism. This is what drives me."—George W. Bush

"If I listened to Michael Dukakis long enough, I would be convinced that we're in an economic downturn and people are homeless and going without food and medical attention and that we've got to do something about the unemployed."
—Ronald Reagan

"To announce that there must be no criticism of the president, or that we are to stand by the president right or wrong is not only unpatriotic and servile, but is morally treasonable to the American public."
—Theodore Roosevelt

"Always be sincere, even if you don't mean it."
—Harry S. Truman

When prompted to say something when turning over a spade of dirt at a ceremonial laying of a cornerstone, Calvin Coolidge said, "That's a fine fish worm."

"The biggest corporation, like the humblest private citizen, must be held to strict compliance with the will of the people."—Teddy Roosevelt, 1900

"My fellow Americans, I've signed legislation that will outlaw Russia forever. We begin bombing in five minutes." —Ronald Reagan, joking just before his radio broadcast, unaware that technicians had already turned on the microphone

"I hold it to be our duty to see that the wage worker, the small producer, the ordinary consumer, shall get their fair share of the benefit of business prosperity." —Teddy Roosevelt, speech to the Ohio Constitutional Convention in 1912

"Where a trust becomes a monopoly, the state has an immediate right to interfere."—Teddy Roosevelt, speech to the New York Legislature, January 3, 1900

"Speak softly and carry a big stick." —Theodore Roosevelt

"No business, which depends for existence on paying less than living wages to its workers, has any right to continue in this country. And, by living wages, I mean more than a bare subsistence. I mean wages for a decent living."—Franklin D. Roosevelt

"FDR was in a wheelchair, and nobody knows. I choke on a pretzel, and the whole world gets to hear about it."—George W. Bush

"The only man who makes no mistake is the man who does nothing." —Theodore Roosevelt

"The business of America is business."
—Calvin Coolidge

"The only thing we have to fear is fear itself."
—Franklin D. Roosevelt, inaugural speech on March 4, 1933, during the Great Depression

"You cannot stop the spread of an idea by passing a law against it."—Harry S. Truman

"I do not think it entirely inappropriate to introduce myself to this audience. I am the man who accompanied Jacqueline Kennedy to Paris, and I have enjoyed it."
—John F. Kennedy, June 1961, when visiting French President Charles de Gaulle and other dignitaries in Paris.

"A government big enough to give you everything you want is a government big enough to take from you everything you have." —Gerald Ford

"I just received the following wire from my generous daddy: 'Dear Jack, Don't buy a single vote more than is necessary. I'll be damned if I'm going to pay for a landslide.'"
—John F. Kennedy

"And so, my fellow Americans, ask not what your country can do for you. Ask what you can do for your country.—John F. Kennedy

"The Democratic Party at its worst is better for the country than the Republican Party at its best."
—Lyndon B. Johnson, 1955

"I'm a great believer in luck, and I find the harder I work the more I have of it."—Thomas Jefferson

"In matters of style, swim with the current; in matters of principle, stand like a rock."—Thomas Jefferson

In 1858 Abraham Lincoln ran against Stephen A. Douglas for election to the Senate. When hearing that Douglas accused Lincoln of being two-faced, Lincoln replied: "If I had another face, do you think I would wear this one?"

"I have always hated slavery."—Abraham Lincoln, 1858

"This nation of ours should not be fearful of faith. We oughta welcome faith to help solve many of the nation's seemingly intractable problems."
—George W. Bush, at a fundraiser in Portland, Oregon, August 24, 2003

When James Madison was gravely ill, a friend begged him not to try to talk while lying in bed. "Oh, I always talk most easily when I lie," Madison replied.

"Even the least informed of the people have learnt that nothing in a newspaper is to be believed...The press ought to be restored to its credibility if possible."—Thomas Jefferson, February 19, 1803, letter to Thomas McKean

"I think that people want peace so much that, one of these days, governments had better get out of their way and let them have it."—Dwight D. Eisenhower, during a television talk with Prime Minister Harold Macmillan of Great Britain, August 31, 1959

"When a great many people are unable to find work, unemployment results."—Calvin Coolidge, discussing the Great Depression

"I think this is the most extraordinary collection of talent, of human knowledge, that has ever been collected together at the White House—with the possible exception of when Thomas Jefferson dined alone."—President John F. Kennedy, at a 1962 White House dinner honoring 49 Nobel Prize winners

"This kind of news conference, where reporters can ask any question they can dream up—directly of the President of the United States—illustrates how strong and how vital our democracy is. There is no other country in the world where the chief of state submits to such unlimited questioning."—Harry S. Truman, after his last press conference

"I am tired of being buffeted in the public prints by a set of infamous scribblers."—George Washington, June 26, 1796, letter to Alexander Hamilton

"Well, I am reading more and enjoying it less."
—John F. Kennedy, when asked on May 9, 1962, how he felt about the press

John F. Kennedy canceled all White House subscriptions to the *New York Herald Tribune*, and when someone used the newspaper to line a box for newborn puppies, Kennedy reportedly said, "It's finally found its proper use."

"Americans learn only from catastrophe and not from experience."—Theodore Roosevelt

"As government expands, liberty contracts."
—Ronald Reagan

"Government does not tax to get the money it needs; government always finds a need for the money it gets."—Ronald Reagan

"A man who has never gone to school may steal from a freight car; but if he has a university education, he may steal the whole railroad."
—Theodore Roosevelt

"History does not long entrust the care of freedom to the weak or the timid."—Dwight D. Eisenhower, January 20, 1953, inaugural address

"To be prepared for war is one of the most effective means of preserving peace."—George Washington

"Government is not reason, it is not eloquence; it is force! Like fire, it is a dangerous servant and a fearful master."—George Washington

"The happiness of society is the end of government." —John Adams

"Few men have virtue to withstand the highest bidder."—George Washington, letter, August 17, 1779

"Liberty, when it begins to take root, is a plant of rapid growth."—George Washington, letter to James Madison, March 2, 1788

"A pen is certainly an excellent instrument to fix a man's attention and to inflame his ambition." —John Adams

"Before I end my letter, I pray heaven to bestow the best of blessings on this house and all that shall hereafter inhabit it. May none but honest and wise men ever rule under this roof."—John Adams, on his second night in the White House, letter to his wife, December 1, 1800

"See, free nations do not develop weapons of mass destruction."—George W. Bush

"The truth is that all men having power ought to be mistrusted."—James Madison

"That government is best which governs the least, because its people discipline themselves."
—Thomas Jefferson

"The price of freedom is eternal vigilance."
—Thomas Jefferson

"The problem to be solved is, not what form of government is perfect, but which of the forms is least imperfect."—James Madison

"National honor is a national property of the highest value."—James Monroe

"The American continents...are henceforth not to be considered as subjects for future colonization by any European powers."—James Monroe, explaining the Monroe Doctrine

"A little flattery will support a man through great fatigue."—James Monroe

"It is easier to do a job right than to explain why you didn't."—Martin Van Buren

"May our country be always successful, but whether successful or otherwise, always right."—John Quincy Adams

"The individual who refuses to defend his rights when called by his government, deserves to be a slave, and must be punished as an enemy of his country and friend to her foe."—Andrew Jackson, September 21, 1841, proclamation to the people of Louisiana from Mobile

"I know what I am fit for. I can command a body of men in a rough way; but I am not fit to be president."—Andrew Jackson

"As to the presidency, the two happiest days of my life were those of my entrance upon the office and my surrender of it."—Martin Van Buren

"I contend that the strongest of all governments is that which is most free."—William Henry Harrison

"A decent and manly examination of the acts of the Government should be not only tolerated, but encouraged."—William Henry Harrison, 1841

"Wealth can only be accumulated by the earnings of industry and the savings of frugality."—William Henry Harrison

"Here lies the body of my good horse, 'The General.' For twenty years he bore me around the circuit of my practice, and in all that time he never made a blunder. Would that his master could say the same!"—John Tyler

"With me it is exceptionally true that the presidency is no bed of roses."—James Knox Polk

"For more than half a century, during which kingdoms and empires have fallen, this Union has stood unshaken. The patriots who formed it have long since descended to the grave; yet still it remains, the proudest monument to their memory."—Zachary Taylor, December 4, 1849, first annual message to Congress

"It is not strange...to mistake change for progress."—Millard Fillmore

"An honorable defeat is better than a dishonorable victory."—Millard Fillmore

"The man who can look upon a crisis without being willing to offer himself upon the altar of his country is not fit for public trust."—Millard Fillmore

"We have nothing in our history or position to invite aggression; we have every reason to cultivate relations of peace and amity with all nations."
—Franklin Pierce

"The ballot box is the surest arbiter of disputes among free men."—James Buchanan

"There is nothing stable but heaven and the Constitution."—James Buchanan

"Common-looking people are the best in the world. That is the reason the Lord makes so many of them."—Abraham Lincoln

"I happen temporarily to occupy this big White House. I am living witness that any one of your children may look to come here as my father's child has."—Abraham Lincoln

"I am rather inclined to silence, and whether that be wise or not, it is at least more unusual nowadays to find a man who can hold his tongue than to find one who cannot."—Abraham Lincoln

"I have stepped out upon this platform that I may see you and that you may see me, and in the arrangement, I have the best of the bargain."
—Abraham Lincoln, campaigning and addressing crowds when stepping off a train platform

"How many legs does a dog have if you call the tail a leg? Four. Calling a tail a leg doesn't make it a leg."
—Abraham Lincoln

"I don't know who my grandfather was; I am much more concerned to know what his grandson will be."—Abraham Lincoln

"Do I not destroy my enemies when I make them my friends?"—Abraham Lincoln

"It is said an Eastern monarch once charged his wise men to invent him a sentence to be ever in view, and which should be true and appropriate in all times and situations. They presented him the words: 'And this, too, shall pass away.'"—Abraham Lincoln

"My experience has taught me that a man who has no vices has damned few virtues."—Abraham Lincoln

"No man has a good enough memory to make a successful liar."—Abraham Lincoln

"Tell me what brand of whiskey that Grant drinks. I would like to send a barrel of it to my other generals."—Abraham Lincoln

"The best way to get a bad law repealed is to enforce it strictly."—Abraham Lincoln

"If the rabble were lopped off at one end and the aristocrat at the other, all would be well with the country."—Andrew Johnson

"Honest conviction is my courage; the Constitution is my guide."—Andrew Johnson

"What we should all work for is a poor government but a rich people."—Andrew Johnson

"Although a soldier by profession, I have never felt any sort of fondness for war, and I have never advocated it except as a means of peace."
—Ulysses S. Grant

"My failures have been errors of judgment, not of intent."—Ulysses S. Grant

"We Americans have no commission from God to police the world."—Benjamin Harrison

"Nothing brings out the lower traits of human nature like office seeking."—Rutherford B. Hayes

"He serves his party best who serves the country best."—Rutherford B. Hayes

"I have had many troubles in my life, but the worst of them never came."—James Garfield

"Whoever controls the volume of money in any country is absolute master of all industry and commerce."—James Garfield

"If it were not for the reporters, I would tell you the truth."—Grover Cleveland

"A man is known by the company he keeps, and also by the company from which he is kept out."
—Grover Cleveland

"Above all, tell the truth."—Grover Cleveland

"In the time of darkest defeat, victory may be nearest."—William McKinley

"The disfranchisement of a single legal elector by fraud or intimidation is a crime too grave to be regarded lightly."—Benjamin Harrison

"Politics: when I am in it, it makes me sick."
—William Howard Taft

"If you want to make enemies, try to change something."—Woodrow Wilson

"Unlike any other nation, here the people rule, and their will is the supreme law. It is sometimes sneeringly said by those who do not like free government, that here we count heads. True, heads are counted, but brains also…"—William McKinley

"Next to the right of liberty, the right of property is the most important individual right guaranteed by the Constitution."—William Howard Taft

"We grow great by dreams. All big men are dreamers."—Woodrow Wilson

"Peace is not made at the council table or by treaties, but in the hearts of men."—Herbert Hoover

"A good leader can't get too far ahead of his followers."—Franklin D. Roosevelt

"Some people call me an idealist. Well, that is the way I know I am an American. America is the only idealist nation in the world."—Woodrow Wilson

"I have never been hurt by anything I didn't say." —Calvin Coolidge

"Character is the only secure foundation of the state."—Calvin Coolidge

"Absolute freedom of the press to discuss public questions is a foundation stone of American liberty." —Herbert Hoover

"Happiness lies in the joy of achievement and the thrill of creative effort."—Franklin D. Roosevelt

"We need not fear the expression of ideas—we do need to fear their suppression."—Harry S. Truman

"A pessimist is one who makes difficulties of his opportunities, and an optimist is one who makes opportunities of his difficulties." —Harry S. Truman

"America is best described by one word, *freedom.*"
—Dwight D. Eisenhower

"I never saw a pessimistic general win a battle."
—Dwight D. Eisenhower

"I don't think the intelligence reports are all that hot.
Some days I get more out of the *New York Times.*"
—John F. Kennedy

"It might be said now that I have the best of both
worlds. A Harvard education and a Yale degree."
—John F. Kennedy, when awarded honorary law
degree, Yale University commencement address,
June 11, 1962

"Should any particular party attempt to abolish Social
Security, unemployment insurance, and eliminate
farm programs, you would not hear of that party
again in our political history. There is a tiny splinter
group, of course, that believes that you can do these
things. Among them are a few Texas oil millionaires
and an occasional politician or business man from

other areas. Their number is negligible, and they are stupid."—Dwight D. Eisenhower

"I believe in an America where religious intolerance will someday end—where all men and all churches are treated as equal—where every man has the same right to attend or not attend the church of his choice...."—John F. Kennedy, speech to the Greater Houston Ministerial Association, September 12, 1960

"Let us never negotiate out of fear. But let us never fear to negotiate."—John F. Kennedy, Inaugural Address, January 20, 1961

"If we cannot end now our differences, at least we can help make the world safe for diversity."
—John F. Kennedy, Commencement Speech at American University, June 10, 1963

"For a closed society is not open to ideas of progress—and a police state finds that it cannot order the grain to grow."—John F. Kennedy, talking about communist states in the State of the Union address, January 14, 1963

"Do you realize the responsibility I carry? I'm the only person standing between Richard Nixon and the White House."—John F. Kennedy, 1960

"Forgive your enemies, but never forget their names."—John F. Kennedy

"[Nikita] Khrushchev reminds me of the tiger hunter who has picked a place on the wall to hang the tiger's skin long before he has caught the tiger. This tiger has other ideas."—John F. Kennedy, speaking of the former premier of the Soviet Union, press conference, June 28, 1961

"As far as I am concerned, now I have no enemies in the press whatsoever."—Richard Nixon, after resigning from the presidency, 1974

"For one priceless moment, in the whole history of man, all the people on this Earth are truly one." —Richard Nixon, to the *Apollo 11* astronauts landing on the moon, July 20, 1969

"Certainly in the next 50 years we shall see a woman president, perhaps sooner than you think. A woman can and should be able to do any political job that a man can do."—Richard Nixon, addressing the League of Women Voters, Washington, D.C., April 16, 1969

"I am not a crook."—Richard Nixon, defending himself during Watergate scandal, November 17, 1973

"I brought myself down. I impeached myself by resigning."—Richard Nixon, television interview with David Frost, May 4, 1977

"We are a nation that has a government—not the other way around. And that makes us special among the nations of the earth."—Ronald Reagan

"I can see clearly now...that I was wrong in not acting more decisively and more forthrightly in dealing with Watergate."—Richard Nixon, response to President Ford's pardon, September 8, 1974

"We declared our independence 200 years ago, and we are not about to lose it now to paper shufflers and computers."—Gerald Ford

"Truth is the glue that holds governments together. Compromise is the oil that makes governments go."—Gerald Ford

"We must adjust to changing times and still hold to unchanging principles."—Jimmy Carter, quoting Julia Coleman, his high school teacher, in his presidential inaugural address, January 20, 1977

"Mr. Gorbachev, tear down this wall."—Ronald Reagan, referring to the Berlin Wall as the symbol of oppression under communism, speech delivered in West Berlin, June 12, 1987

"The best way to enhance freedom in other lands is to demonstrate here that our democratic system is worthy of emulation."—Jimmy Carter, inaugural address, January 20, 1977

"I've got a foreign policy that is one that believes America has a responsibility in this world to lead."
—George W. Bush, interview on television show *Meet the Press*, February 9, 2004

"America is too great for small dreams."
—Ronald Reagan, 1984

"The taxpayer: That's someone who works for the federal government but doesn't have to take the civil service examination."—Ronald Reagan

"Government is like a baby: an alimentary canal with a big appetite at one end and no sense of responsibility at the other."—Ronald Reagan

"No arsenal, or no weapon in the arsenals of the world, is so formidable as the will and moral courage of free men and women."—Ronald Reagan

"If anyone tells you that America's best days are behind her, they're looking the wrong way."
—George H. W. Bush, State of the Union speech, January 29, 1991

"The United States is the best and fairest and most decent nation on the face of the earth."
—George H. W. Bush

"Don't try to fine-tune somebody else's view."
—George H. W. Bush

"I want a kinder, gentler nation."—George H. W. Bush, on accepting the Republican party's nomination for president, Republican National Convention, New Orleans, August 18, 1988

"There is nothing wrong in America that can't be fixed with what is right in America."—Bill Clinton

"In the councils of government, we must guard against the acquisition and unwarranted influence, whether sought or unsought, by the military-industrial complex. The potential for the disastrous rise of misplaced power exists and will persist. We must never let the weight of this combination endanger our liberties or democratic processes."
—Dwight D. Eisenhower, farewell address to the nation, before leaving office, January 17, 1961

On Manners and Motives

As a schoolboy, George Washington hand copied 110 rules of civility that had been compiled by French Jesuits in 1595 and translated into English in 1640. In his adult life, Washington kept these rules in mind. Here are a few: "Every action done in company ought to be with some sign of respect, to those that are present." "In the presence of others sing not to yourself with a humming noise, nor drum with your fingers or feet."

Abraham Lincoln reportedly framed and hung on his office wall these wise sayings he composed: "If I tried to read, much less answer, all the attacks made on me, this shop might as well be closed for any other business. I do the very best I know how; the very best I can. I mean to keep doing so down to the very end. If the end brings me out all right, what is said against me won't amount to anything. If the end brings me out wrong, then ten angels swearing I was right would make no difference."

On Term Limits

James Polk, Andrew Johnson, Rutherford B. Hayes, and Grover Cleveland did not favor the idea of a president running for office a second time. In 1915, President William Howard Taft believed that a single term would give the president greater courage and independence since he would not have to worry about how his decisions could affect his re-election.

Lyndon B. Johnson's Humor

Lyndon B. Johnson may have been one of the most humorous presidents. Most of his quotes are funny. Some fall into the "might have said" category. These include:

"You ain't learnin' nothin' when you're talkin'."

"The fact that a man is a newspaper reporter is evidence of some flaw of character."

"Being president is like being a jackass in a hailstorm. There's nothing to do but to stand there and take it."

"He's [Gerald Ford] a nice guy, but he played too much football with his helmet off."

"I have learned that only two things are necessary to keep one's wife happy. First, let her think she's having her own way. And second, let her have it."

"I want to make a policy statement. I am unabashedly in favor of women."

"If one morning I walked on top of the water across the Potomac River, the headline that afternoon would read: 'President Can't Swim.'"

Chapter 12
Presidents Before and After

Is there life after being president of the United States? Most of the presidents who survived the office would probably answer yes. Many became richer when they left the Oval Office and joined the speaking circuit or entered the offices of their New York publishers. Some, like Jimmy Carter, became more influential in world events after their presidency. Others, like Ronald Reagan, seemed destined for the highest office by dint of exceptional success in earlier careers. Greatness, it seems, is portable.

"Politics is not a bad profession. If you succeed, there are many rewards. If you disgrace yourself, you can always write a book."—Ronald Reagan

After leaving the Presidency in 1829, John Quincy Adams was elected to the House of Representatives. He served from 1831 until his death in 1848.

Although he declined the appointment, in 1849, Abraham Lincoln was offered the position of Governor of the Oregon Territory.

President Grover Cleveland was the first movie-star president. In April of 1895, Alexander Black came to Washington, D.C., to convince Cleveland to appear in his photoplay *A Capital Courtship*. The president agreed to be photographed while signing a bill into law.

President Millard Fillmore spent several years of his young adulthood as an apprentice to a cloth maker.

After leaving the presidency in 1913, William Howard Taft went on to become chief justice of the Supreme Court. He served from 1921 until his death in 1930.

At the age of fifteen, Lyndon B. Johnson ran away from home and traveled to California, where he worked as a grape picker and auto mechanic.

There have been fourteen presidents who first served as vice presidents—John Adams, Thomas Jefferson, Martin Van Buren, John Tyler, Millard Fillmore, Andrew Johnson, Chester A. Arthur, Teddy Roosevelt, Calvin Coolidge, Harry S. Truman, Richard Nixon, Lyndon B. Johnson, Gerald Ford, and George H. W. Bush.

George W. Bush was head cheerleader at his prep school in 1964. The list of former cheerleaders includes GOP presidents Ronald Reagan and Dwight D. Eisenhower. All of this made *Gentlemen's Quarterly* magazine writer Jim Nelson develop his Grand Cheerleader Theory. Cheerleaders become Republicans, who in turn become our nation's leaders.

In 1940, young actor Ronald Reagan got his big break—playing the role of Notre Dame football legend, George Gipp, in the film *Knute Rockne, All American*. He appeared in 53 films and became president of the Screen Actors Guild (1947–1952, 1959–1960).

In 1782, toward the end of the American Revolution, General George Washington reacted strongly against the idea circulating in the Army to make him King. Washington said, "No occurrence in the course of the War has given me more painful sensations."

John Adams was a writer and a schoolteacher, lawyer, diplomat, and vice president under George Washington before becoming president.

Thomas Jefferson was an inventor, lawyer, an architect, governor of Virginia, secretary of state under Washington, and vice president under John Adams. After leaving office, he did what most presidents do. He went back to being a writer. He was also a gentleman farmer and rector at the University of Virginia.

At age 19, George H. W. Bush was the youngest combat pilot in the Navy during World War II. He flew 58 missions before being shot down by Japanese anti-aircraft fire in the Pacific. After spending hours in shark-infested waters, Bush was rescued by a U.S. submarine.

Abraham Lincoln had a thriving law practice in Springfield, Illinois. He was a corporate lawyer for railroad and canal companies and charged fees of up to $5,000 for his services.

In the late 1940s, future president Ronald Reagan became an FBI informant in an effort to purge communists from Hollywood unions.

As a young man, James A. Garfield wanted to be a professional sailor and worked on a canal boat.

Richard Nixon was once a barker for a *Wheel-of-Chance* game at a Prescott, Arizona, rodeo. The Slippery Gulch Rodeo was a front for a backroom gambling operation.

In tribute to his contributions to botanical science, a plant was named after Thomas Jefferson—*Jeffersonia diphylla*.

Harry S. Truman worked as a timekeeper for the Santa Fe railroad.

Gerald Ford was once a male model.

James A. Garfield was a professor of Latin and Greek at Hiram College in Ohio.

John Quincy Adams was once ambassador to Prussia (now part of Germany and Poland).

James K. Polk was the only president to have previously been speaker of the House.

Dwight D. Eisenhower served as president of Columbia University after World War II and prior to running for the U.S. presidency.

Woodrow Wilson was once president of Princeton University.

As a young man, Herbert Hoover managed gold-mining operations overseas.

Before the presidency, Warren G. Harding worked as a newspaper publisher and editor.

During his college days, Dwight D. Eisenhower played semi-professional baseball. He used an assumed name (Wilson) to avoid losing his eligibility to play college football.

Lyndon B. Johnson began his career as a schoolteacher and principal before going to Washington in 1931 to become the secretary to Congressman Richard Kleburg. Four years later, Johnson was appointed director of the National Youth Administration (NYA) in Texas. The purpose of the NYA was to provide education, jobs, recreation, and counseling for male and female youths, ages 16 to 25. Johnson scholars recognize the seeds of his Great Society in his early involvement in the NYA.

As a boy, Theodore Roosevelt watched Abraham Lincoln's funeral procession from an upstairs window of his grandfather's house on Union Square, New York City. With him were his younger brother Elliott and a friend named Edith Kermit Carow.

In 1882, Theodore Roosevelt published his first book, *The Naval War of 1812*, written partly while he was in college. The book set the standard for studies on naval strategy and was required reading at the Naval Academy in Annapolis for many years.

In 1895, just before he became president, Theodore Roosevelt served as New York City Police Commissioner. Between 1895 and 1897, Theodore Roosevelt received national press attention for his reforms, including "midnight rambles" in search of policemen not at their posts. He ordered that all police officers report for target practice, thus establishing the foundation of the Police Academy, one of the first in the country.

In 1909, during his presidency, Theodore Roosevelt published *Outdoor Pastimes of an American Hunter*—a best-seller and one of the first books about the great outdoors.

Ronald Reagan served as a lifeguard several summers in his youth. Reagan claimed to have saved 77 people from drowning.

Dwight D. Eisenhower participated in the first cross-country truck convoy.

Thomas Jefferson was the nation's first secretary of state.

During World War II, George H. W. Bush received the Distinguished Flying Cross after being shot down in his Grumman Avenger during a bombing raid on the island of Chichi Jima. He stayed afloat on a life raft until a submarine rescued him.

Before embarking on his professional career as a lawyer, young Abraham Lincoln joined the militia to fight Chief Black Hawk of the Sauk tribe.

After leaving the presidency, Theodore Roosevelt led hunting expeditions to Africa to gather specimens for the Smithsonian Institution.

William McKinley was in charge of the food supplies for his brigade during the Civil War. His commanding officer reported, "From his hands every man in the regiment was served with hot coffee and warm meats, a thing that had never occurred under similar circumstances in any other army in the world." The commanding officer was Rutherford B. Hayes, later to become president.

Theodore Roosevelt became famous for leading his Rough Riders to San Juan Hill in Cuba, a decisive battle during the Spanish-American War in 1898.

On August 2, 1943, John F. Kennedy was lost at sea in the Pacific, after an enemy (Japanese) ship sliced through the ship he commanded. He was eventually rescued from the waters.

Lyndon B. Johnson was decorated with the Silver Star for gallantry under enemy fire. General Douglas MacArthur bestowed the honor on Johnson.

Grover Cleveland was a sheriff of Erie County, New York. During that time, he personally carried out the hangings of two convicted murderers.

During World War II, Ronald Reagan made motion pictures for the military. He was called up as a member of the army reserve and rose to the rank of captain, refusing a promotion to major.

Theodore Roosevelt won the Nobel Peace Prize in 1906 for his role as peacemaker in the Russo-Japanese War. Woodrow Wilson won it in 1920 for his efforts in seeking a just peace after World War I and in supporting the idea of the League of Nations. Former president Jimmy Carter was the last to win it, in 2002.

Both George H. W. Bush and Herbert Hoover lived in China before becoming president. Bush was at the U.S. Liaison Office in Beijing, and Hoover worked as chief engineer of China's bureau of mines.

Future president Richard Nixon once said of then current president Lyndon B. Johnson that "...we both have a lot in common. We both served in the House. We both served in the Senate. We both served as vice president. We both ran for president against John F. Kennedy—and lost!"

Benjamin Harrison almost became a physician. In the late 18th century, it took only two 16-week courses to receive a medical degree, but Harrison dropped out of the University of Pennsylvania before completing his studies.

After graduating from Williams College in Massachusetts, future president James A. Garfield became a professor of classical languages at Hiram College in Ohio.

William Howard Taft was asked to become the governor of the Philippines under President William McKinley during the guerilla war that followed the Spanish-American War.

William Howard Taft said that the greatest honor of his life was not having served as president, but his appointment as chief justice to the Supreme Court.

Index

343

ABOUT THE AUTHOR

Glen Vecchione is the author of fifteen books for Sterling Publishing Co., Inc., distributed worldwide. Some Sterling titles have been reprinted by Scholastic, and others have been translated into Spanish and other languages and reprinted by foreign publishers.

When he's not writing, Glen uses his talents as a software engineer, web designer, and musical composer of television jingles and more serious works. He also enjoys dabbling in playwriting and acting. With Quiet Zone Theatre, an Orange County-based company of hearing-impaired actors and dancers, Glen adapted the Dr. Seuss book *Bartholomew & the Oobleck* for American Sign Language. His one-act play *Cowboy BO & the Train Whistle* premiered in San Diego in 2006. Abstract expressionist painting is one of his passions. Another is shopping for tasteful Hawaiian shirts.

ACKNOWLEDGMENTS

Our thanks to Lee Finkle, Ph.D., retired professor of American history from Indiana University, Hunter College, and Pace University, for vetting this book.